CHANEL

CHANEL

by
Jean Leymarie

Abrams, New York

CONTENTS

THE LEGEND OF CHANEL   7

1   COSTUME, FASHION, AND HAUTE COUTURE   9

2   OBAZINE AND ROYALLIEU   39

3   CHANEL MODES   45

4   DEAUVILLE AND BIARRITZ   53

5   THE JERSEY REVOLUTION   59

6   ENCOUNTERS   65

7   PERFUMES   83

8   EMBROIDERY   91

9   ANTIGONE AND LE TRAIN BLEU   97

10   ELEGANCE AND SIMPLICITY   111

11   ORPHÉE   123

12   VARIATIONS AND CURVES   129

13   LONDON   141

14   HOLLYWOOD   147

15   HOMES AND INTERIORS   157

16   VENICE   173

17   JEWELRY   179

18   SOPHISTICATION AND SPECTACLE   195

19   RETIREMENT   219

20   RETURN AND RECOGNITION   223

21   INFLUENCE AND LEGACY   241

INDEX OF ILLUSTRATIONS   249

THE LEGEND OF CHANEL

This book in no way claims to replace the biographies that have been written about the woman known to her friends as Coco, nor to provide the systematic and specialized study that remains to be written about the oeuvre of the legendary Mademoiselle Chanel. Its selection and sequence of illustrations are designed to provide a general overview of Chanel's creative history and evolution within the context of the artistic world of her time. Gabrielle Chanel never confused the practice of couture—which she clearly perceived as a profession, a craft, and a trade—with the work of the great artists who had become her friends and her mentors. Nonetheless, she ruled over the domain of fashion, around the world, with the same supremacy her contemporary Pablo Picasso had over the domain of painting. Above all Chanel, like Picasso, had the rare ability to crystallize around her name and her undertakings a myth that still endures today.

Her success was a result of the conjunction of her personal gifts and a set of circumstances she seized upon with an infallible sense of flair, as well as the energy that she brought to bear on managing her business affairs, expressing her tastes, and attaining her destiny. Her greatest and most important creations in her own realm and related fields—jewelry, perfumes, interior decoration, theater, and film—form part of the broader wake of her illustrious lifestyle and her personal influence as a hostess and a patron of the arts.

She cut a broad swath through the times in which she lived, and marked them deeply with her imprint. Because she was the very embodiment of a new kind of woman, in style, looks and behavior, she had a thorough understanding of the places where modern women lived, both at home and on vacation, and was able to design—first and foremost for herself—suitable clothing that she herself popularized. "I invented sportswear for myself," she used to say, "not because other women were fond of sports, but because I was. I didn't succeed because I needed to create fashion; I created fashion precisely because I was succeeding, because I was the first to live the life of the century."

In her age and in the rigor of her style, she belonged to the illustrious generation of the Cubists, of whom she knew all the major figures—painters, sculptors, musicians, and poets—who will be discussed below. In order to define the true role she played and the importance of the revolution she began, we will need to indulge in a brief summary of the history of fashion: its age-old glamour and the modern significance of Haute Couture.

Gabrielle Chanel in 1937.
Photograph by Sir Cecil Beaton.

1

COSTUME, FASHION, AND HAUTE COUTURE

Offering Bearer. From Assiut, Egypt,
Middle Kingdom, Eleventh Dynasty
(2100–2000 BCE). Painted and stuccoed
woodcarving.

The word "costume" is closely related to the word "custom," and the two concepts are intertwined, inasmuch as donning a costume, or any item of clothing, is tantamount to subjecting one's external appearance to the expectations of society. The importance of clothing extends well beyond the three basic functions that are generally associated with it (at times with a degree of ambivalence): physical protection, modesty, and adornment. It is also a significant factor in defining relationships between human beings and their natural and social environments. It is possible to divide apparel into two fundamental types, which are often found in conjunction: draped garments, generally Mediterranean in origin, and stitched garments, for the most part from northern lands. The history of clothing in the West can be divided into three broad periods. From early antiquity up to the Middle Ages, impersonal forms of apparel, common to both genders, remained relatively stable and codified, retaining a sense of their magical or religious significance.

In the fourteenth century, with the metamorphosis of costume and the differentiation between male and female apparel, the mysterious force of fashion, which cannot be reduced to its separate and component causes, brought a series of national shifts and changes, with individual variations within each social hierarchy. In the ongoing period since the middle of the nineteenth century, fashion has become an autonomous system that aims to rule the entire planet by means of the opposing but allied forces of industrial mass production and specialized Haute Couture.

It is, however, impossible to separate costume or clothing from the person who wears it and thus takes on its symbolic value. It is equally impossible to ignore the manner in which clothing is perceived in the context of different art forms, among them (in the modern day) photography and film. This phenomenon can be traced back to the ancient civilizations that flourished around the Mediterranean Basin, which continue to this day to yield their cultural treasures to archaeological excavations. Those civilizations shared a common trait in the sphere of clothing: draped, diaphanous fabric with harmonious folds that flattered the proportions of the human body. These fabrics were woven by virgins and presented in processions at the Parthenon as an offering to Athena, protectress of the city named after her. Ancient Egypt holds a particularly strong attraction for our modern sensibilities, with the hieratic power and lithe grace of its art. The *Offering-Bearer* at the Louvre (Middle Kingdom, Eleventh Dynasty) is one of a group of priceless painted wooden sculptures depicting craftsmen and peasants at work, created for placement in underground shrines. This young female figure walks with sober elegance toward the tomb of her lord, with a vessel of water in one hand and a basket filled with provisions from her farm balanced on her head, topped by a leg of beef. Her body is sheathed in a close-fitting dress fastened over the shoulders by two slender straps, leaving her breasts uncovered; at her neckline is an ornamental collar. The dress must actually have been more loose-fitting than it appears here; otherwise it would have been difficult for her to walk freely. Its tight fit, so striking and attractive to our modern sensibilities, reflects sculptural conventions whereby clothing clung closely to the body. The dress is made of linen covered with multicolored meshwork in leather or beads. Wool, by contrast, was considered impure, because it came from animals. It was therefore banned from use in temples and funeral ceremonies. Linen, light and cool, was well suited to the Egyptian climate; it was preferred because of its natural whiteness and its sacred nature.

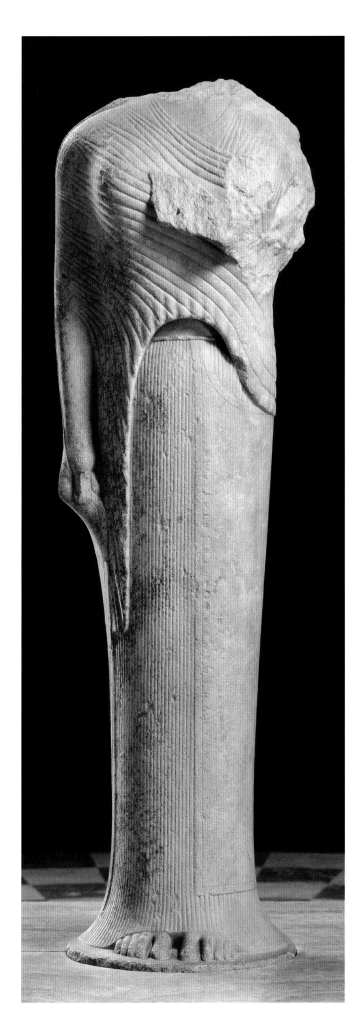

The ancient Greeks emphasized the sculptural magnificence of the human body through the contrast between drapery and bare skin. Women wore two chief articles of clothing: either the Doric *peplos*, a woolen rectangle with its upper hems folded over and clasped with shoulder brooches, or the Ionic *chiton*, a linen tunic of Egyptian origin, stitched up the sides. There is a large marble statue at the Louvre dedicated to the sanctuary of Hera, on the Ionian island of Samos; this sculpture, with its distinctly Eastern pose, heralds the evocative style of the archaic Kore, a feminine votive statue. It has the majesty of a tree-like pillar, combining organic fluidity and abstract rigor. The statue is missing both its left arm and its head; the right arm hangs loosely. Three distinct articles of clothing—tunic, cape, and veil—enfold the perfect body of the stately goddess, bride of Zeus, whose forms curve and blossom beneath the harmonious movements of the fabrics, with their smooth or textured surfaces, either with broad diagonal folds or fine vertical and parallel ridges.

The Kore of Samos.
First half of the sixth century BCE.

BESIDES, TRUE BEAUTY IS STRICTLY IMPOSSIBLE TO DESCRIBE: BEFORE THESE STATUES ONE MAY SPEAK OF STYLE; ONE MAY SPEAK OF HUMANITY, OF GRANDEUR, OF SIMPLICITY, ONE MAY SPEAK OF TRUTH, OF REALISM. BUT THIS COULD BE SAID OF ALL THE STATUARY OF THIS PERIOD, WHICH IS UNIQUE AND CANNOT BE CONFUSED WITH ANY OTHER. AND IN THE DEPTHS OF MY UNCONSCIOUS I SEARCH FOR SOMETHING THAT WILL ENABLE ME TO SAY WHAT IT IS ABOUT THESE STATUES THAT MAKES THEM UNIQUE AND TRULY UNLIKE ANYTHING ELSE EVEN AMONG THIS UNIQUE STATUARY. I LOOK FOR THAT PARTICULAR NOTE OF HUMANITY OR REALISM THAT COMBINES EXALTATION AND TENDERNESS, SIMPLIFICATION AND SUMPTUOUSNESS. THESE STATUES WERE CARVED BY A STRONG AND GENTLE HAND WHICH TOLD ALL BUT ADMITTED NOTHING. THEY ARE BOTH SYNTHETIC AND PARTICULAR, AND THE PARTICULAR STORY THAT THEY TELL SEEMS TO BE OF TIME ARRESTED IN ITS FLIGHT. FROM THEIR UNDEFINABLE POETRY THEY SEEM TO DRAW A VERY ODD MIXTURE OF STYLE AND IMMEDIATE PRESENCE.

Antonin Artaud

The frescoes of the Villa of the Mysteries, discovered in the spring of 1909 in Pompeii, show the late Greek style of painting transposed to Italian soil during the reign of Augustus. These frescoes depict an architectural space within which are portrayed, in a continual frieze along the walls of the room, a succession of unsettling scenes from an initiation into the practices of the Dionysian cult. The intense figure of a matron, shown here in isolation, marks the beginning of the series of frescoes. This mature woman stands motionless at the threshold of the secret chamber where women officiated. One hand on her hip, the other holding her veil, she listens intently as a young boy reads the ritual aloud (in the scene that follows).

This solemn and intimate figure, so close to the viewer, poised on the green marble pediment, reaches out to us with the unusual realism of her face, the pensive concentration evident in her posture, the circumspect dignity of her gestures, and the lively spontaneity of this pictorial style with its original Campanian accents. The costume's colors and nuances of light and shade—the delicate veil covering her hair and torso, the heavy, rich *peplos* with broad fluted folds that cascade to the floor—stand out magnificently against the vivid red background that is characteristic of the Villa and the style of Pompeii.

The Roman costume, derived from the Greek tunic and the Etruscan toga, spread throughout Europe and lasted for many centuries, in both a long version worn by the upper classes and a shorter version worn by soldiers and laborers. The Crusaders' expeditions to the Middle East accelerated the spread of Eastern silks and other luxury fabrics brought back to Europe through Venice, Moorish Spain, and Saracen Sicily. These fabrics also encouraged the development of a tradition of courtly lyricism that enumerated a lady's charms by describing the exquisite refinements of her apparel. The songs and verses of chivalry and the love poetry of the Provencal troubadours overlapped, despite their different sources, with the Marian cult exalted in Gothic art. We can trace the development of that style over a number of decades, from a supernatural majesty to a graceful contrapposto.

The Initiate, detail.
Fresco, Villa of the Mysteries,
Pompeii. c. 60–70 BCE.

Countess Uta of Naumburg,
c. 1260. Naumburg Cathedral.

The statues commemorating the founders of the cathedral of Naumburg, Germany, erected around 1260 in the choir of that cathedral, do not fit in with the liturgical program or the architectural constraints of their setting. Full-fledged medieval portraits, they exert a powerful effect on modern viewers with their eloquent and powerful features and their strange grandeur, at once gentle and sublime. The noble face of the Countess Uta, beneath her heraldic crown, bears an unmistakable expression of both spiritual fervor and palpable seductiveness. She raises the collar of her cape to cover her cheek, in an exquisite gesture of simultaneous flirtation and modesty. The colorful grain of the stone allows us to glimpse one delicate hand beneath the tautly stretched fabric and the sumptuous spiral of drapery clasped by the other hand. The fashion photographer and close friend of Gabrielle Chanel, Horst P. Horst, many of whose pictures appear in this book, admired this extraordinary statue from an early age (his birthplace was close to Naumburg). In his eyes, the Countess Uta was the incarnation of ideal beauty. Diana Vreeland, the great American fashion expert and editor of *Vogue*, was equally close to the famed French designer and had a reproduction of Countess Uta in her office, considering her to be a supreme and timeless symbol of feminine elegance.

During the middle of the fourteenth century, newly rediscovered aesthetic ideals of elegance and beauty governed the code of ethics of the aristocracy, at the advent of a revolution in apparel that ushered in the power of what may henceforth be described as fashion. It was then that men and women abandoned the old style of loose, undifferentiated garments and adopted a new kind of fitted clothing that drew a clear distinction between the sexes and their respective sensual qualities. Men adopted short outfits, with separated legs, tight-fitting hose, and a padded doublet. Women remained in long dresses, but these dresses now clung to the upper body, slimming the waist and revealing the shoulders and throat through the audacious contrivance of the décolleté, or low neckline. This transformation of the silhouette required a number of technical advances in the weaving and cutting of garments, which were also laced and buttoned. Sumptuary laws had to be issued to regulate the use of fabrics and prohibit the bourgeoisie, then flourishing with the development of trade, from gaining access to the sartorial privileges of the nobility.

Fashion at its dawn—in the modern sense, as the dynamic and stylistic aspect of apparel—was also at its most enchanting. Frescoes, illuminations, tapestries, and books of designs and sketches created by the masters of the workshops (who proved to be the first and magnificent fashion designers) give us a sense of the feminine fairyland of the International Gothic school. One of the earliest collections—dating even before the anthologies of Pisanello, so renowned for their creative and innovative costumes—is now attributed to Giovannino de' Grassi, a painter, architect, and sculptor who was active between 1389 and 1398 at Visconti Castle in Milan. (He was working for the ancestors of the Italian filmmaker Luchino Visconti, who was so sensitive to the magic of costumes, and who was a protégé of Chanel at the beginning of his career.) De' Grassi's collection includes fine watercolor studies of plants, animals, emblems, and delightful figures of musicians in their flowing garments.

France and the urban principalities of northern Italy were the leading centers of the courtly movement of Humanism. Aristocratic life moved to the rhythms of dance and music and was entirely conceived as a grand spectacle. The duchy of Burgundy, which based its wealth on the flourishing silk and woolens industries, built its prestige upon the luxuriousness of its costumes and its festivities.

The links between art and fashion were strengthened during the Renaissance. In the sixteenth century, portraiture was the dominant art form. To Hans Holbein, Bronzino, and Titian, who all claimed aesthetic independence in terms of form, material, and color, a costume had value not only as an emblem of social standing, but also as a revealing indicator of an individual's psychology and taste. Great nations took shape, successors to the feudal principalities. As they did, fashion reflected these political changes. Following a phase of fertile interaction between Italy and France, who dazzled one another with their costumes and customs, Spain gained supremacy in the realm of apparel.

While Charles V was attending the Diet of Augsburg in 1548, he summoned Titian to wait on him, and it was probably there that, using some likeness, Titian painted, or repainted, this portrait of the Empress Isabella. She had died young, in 1539, and the Emperor wished to have an imperishable likeness of her by the greatest painter of the day. Her noble beauty and natural distinction are enhanced by the brocades and jewelry she is wearing. During his stay in Genoa in the mid-1620s, Van Dyck painted his great series of Baroque portraits of the local aristocracy, of which this is one. The fine face and hands of the marchioness are set off by the rich hues of the famous Genoese velvets of that period. The palatial setting of hanging and columns harmonizes perfectly with her noble bearing and gorgeous costume.

Diego Velázquez (1599–1660)
The Infanta Maria Theresa, c. 1653.
Oil on canvas.

Reacting against the loose and colorful forms that had gone before, Spain imposed a rigid and severe style for women, with a geometric structure: a high bodice and a bell-shaped petticoat with wooden or metal hoops, the so-called *verdugado* or farthingale, the predecessor of panniers and crinolines. By the seventeenth century, the guiding criterion in the realm of apparel was no longer individual elegance, as it had been during the Renaissance or the Mannerist phase, but rather social hierarchy and the preservation of decorum. Each class and each profession had its own distinctive way of dressing. This can be seen in a comparison of the portrait of Isabel of Portugal by Titian and the portrait of the Marchesa Doria by Anthony Van Dyck; the latter brought new life to the genre by placing the subject within a setting of trees and pillars, marking the transition from being to seeming and, in terms of the treatment of fabrics, from the interplay of colors to the effects of light.

After creating portraits of jesters and dwarfs, now in the Prado, Diego Velázquez used a palette of exquisite floral hues to paint the *Infantas* series, currently found in the Kunsthistorisches Museum in Vienna. The eldest daughter of Philippe IV and the radiant jewel of his court, Maria Theresa was fourteen or fifteen years old when she posed for the portrait illustrated, in the blossom of her youth and dressed in finery befitting her high station. Against the dark green and velvet-blue background, her monumental costume is an ethereal confection of grays and silvers, punctuated by the pearly sheen of her jewelry and the pink of the ribbons and trimmings. From that stately cage that has become a halo of light, we see emerging, in a miracle of verisimilitude and a marvel of painterly skill, the fine complexion of her hands and the iconic expression of her face beneath the opulent hairstyle. Here the costume truly serves as the glorious fabric of the painting and provides a ceremonial aura of beauty.

SINCE PAINTING IS MEANT TO REVEAL A SPIRITUAL WORLD, IT NEEDS A MATERIAL RICH IN POSSIBILITIES FOR INCARNATION. WHEN VELAZQUEZ PAINTED AN INFANTA, HE PAINTED A PORTRAIT, THE PORTRAIT OF A LITTLE GIRL WITH A MATTE COMPLEXION, BUT HER ADMIRABLE GOWN ALSO INDICATED A RANK, A SOCIAL FUNCTION, AND SUGGESTED A SORT OF SACREDNESS THAT IS ALWAYS EXPRESSED BY COSTUME.

Balthus

Maria Theresa was married to Louis XIV in 1660, and it was during
his reign that France regained uncontested sway over the realm of
fashion for the century that followed. Antoine Watteau was, like
Pisanello, an unrivaled draftsman and a skilled portrayer of costume. He did not invent the pleated "Watteau dress" that bears
his name, but he did convey its magic, a charm that Chanel and
other couturiers tried on several occasions to revive. His dreamlike
world emerges from the life drawings that he called his *pensées*,
or thoughts. He liked to depict figures from the back, so as best
to evoke a sense of poetic suggestion and to show, beneath the
curve of the nape of the neck, the cascade of folds and pleats falling from the shoulders to the floor. The *trois crayons* sketch at the
Teylers Museum in Haarlem is one of the preparatory drawings for
his masterpiece, now at Dulwich Picture Gallery, *Les Plaisirs du bal*
(Pleasures of the Ball), painted around 1717. William Turner copied
this painting and John Constable said that it seemed to have been
"painted in honey: so mellow, so tender, so soft, and so delicious."
The young woman wearing a toque is lifting the skirts of her dress
beneath her cape as she prepares to dance.

This *robe volante* or sack dress, which hung loosely around the body,
was in fashion during the Régence period; during the reign of Louis XV,
it became the *robe à la française*, fitted at the waist, and was famously
worn by the Marquise de Pompadour. The king's official mistress from
1745 to 1750, Madame de Pompadour became the arbiter of elegance
and a patron of the arts. Educated in salon society, she was both witty
and literate, and gave her support to the finest writers of her time as
well as the publication of the *Encyclopédie* of Denis Diderot and Jean
le Rond d'Alembert, in which the subjects of fashion and the textiles
trade were given full attention. Portraits of Madame de Pompadour,
many of which were painted by François Boucher, depict her in the
interiors or grounds of her various residences, which she managed
and decorated with unerring taste. Sleeves with flounces and lace,
ribbon trimmings, and a ladder of bows down the bodice are among
the charming adornments that were, in the words of Diderot, "the
true domain of imagination and transformation."

Antoine Watteau (1684–1721)
*Standing Woman, from Behind, About to
Start Dancing*, c. 1717.
Red, black, and white chalk.

François Boucher (1703–1770)
The Marquise de Pompadour, 1759.
Oil on canvas.

Francisco Goya's portrait of the Countess of Carpio, Marquesa de la Solana, was the centerpiece of the Beistegui collection, which Chanel saw in Biarritz before it was transferred to the Louvre. This portrait marked the artist's departure from the florid style of Boucher. Goya rejected embellishment, ignored social standing, and focused only on depicting a human being in all her intimacy and austerity. Pierre Gassier, a noted Goya scholar, once wrote, "No other work by Goya better expresses the melancholy pride of the Spanish soul."

This portrait was painted shortly before the model's death in 1795. The countess was an intelligent, passionate woman and a close friend of the artist, whose liberal beliefs she shared. She wished to leave her only daughter a standing portrait of herself. It shows her erect and firm, turned at a three-quarter angle, her body frail but intent with proud determination. Her dark eyes burn fervently in the oval of her face, with its sensual mouth. There are two hints of color: the ivory fan and the dusky pink of the ribbons on her chestnut, almost auburn, hair, brightening the black-and-gray harmony of her costume, a dark, straight dress with a light-colored lace mantilla. Her little shoes are also black and gray, crossed like her gloved hands. This stark and vibrant silhouette stands out against the bare background, with floor and wall all the same hue.

Jacques-Louis David, who designed costumes during the French Revolution and the subsequent French Empire, was Goya's exact contemporary. The two artists, so different in temperament, were nonetheless similar in the freedom of their vision and their confident mastery of their craft.

Francisco Goya (1746–1828)
Countess of Carpio, Marquesa de la Solana, c. 1794.
Oil on canvas.

Jacques-Louis David (1748–1825)
Madame Récamier, 1800 (unfinished).
Oil on canvas.

Goya had the love of black that was so typical of Spain, while David cultivated a neoclassical taste for white muslin and for the *robes de simplicité* ("dresses of simplicity") that were prevalent at the time. Juliette Récamier was in the bloom of youth when David, in May or June of 1800, captured the quintessential pose in which the irresistible and mysterious beauty would be seen for the rest of her life—half-reclining, torso erect, on her classical-style chaise. The chaise depicted here was not her own; it was a more restrained design in bronze and mahogany, likewise made by the Jacob brothers, that the painter kept as furnishing in his studio. Her hair is up and her bare feet are on display. Her white gown, to which she remained faithful although it was no longer in fashion, reveals the perfection of her form and yet creates a distance with its virginal purity. The thin vertical line of the tall torchère (which may have been painted by Jean Auguste Dominique Ingres, who was at the time a pupil of David) sets off the diagonal curve of the subject and the supple tension of her body against the blue and yellow cushions.

The floor and the wall are little more than gray and brown smears. The painting, intentionally left unfinished, is admirable for its masterly workmanship and its complex artistic expressiveness.

Jean Auguste Dominique Ingres (1780–1867)
Madame de Senonnes, 1814.
Oil on canvas.

Jean Auguste Dominique Ingres (1780–1867)
Study for the dress of Baroness James de Rothschild. Black and white chalk on brown paper.

Ingres was the last painter of genius who was able to fulfill commissions for portraits without betraying his own style. His gallery of high-society women is a succession of triumphs and a seminal documentation of the array of costumes in fashion at the turn and the middle of the nineteenth century. Honoré de Balzac introduced descriptions of apparel into his novels—"the most forceful of symbols," as he put it. Charles Baudelaire, who was sensitive to the artifice and the magic of fashion, declared, "What poet would dare, in a painting of the pleasure caused by the appearance of a beauty, separate the woman from her clothing?"

Ingres's *Portrait of Madame de Senonnes*, painted in 1814 and widely considered to be his best portrait, is the first work in which the artist makes use, in his own style, of the age-old device of the mirror. The preliminary sketches show that the original pose, modified over the course of the painting's execution, was much closer to that of David's *Madame Récamier*. Ingres differed from his teacher in the vital importance that he placed not on the drawing of contours, but rather on the line itself as a generator of form and movement. His portraits bring together his concern with realism and his capacity for abstraction. Madame de Senonnes is sitting on a yellow silk couch, wearing a dark-red velvet dress. Her languorous curves form part of the spiral rhythm of the composition, which entails the foreshortening of the left arm and the elongation of the right arm.

The three-tiered lace collar, the ruches of tulle, the numerous rings, the cluster of pendants, and the twisting lengths of the Indian shawl embroidered with flowers (a vital accessory that would have cost more than the dress itself)—all this unostentatious profusion is incorporated into the mellow atmosphere of the boudoir and enhanced by the reflective interplay of the mirror.

The Comtesse d'Haussonville marked the beginning, in 1845, of a new series of aristocratic beauties of whom Ingres was commissioned to paint portraits, despite his own artistic preferences. The Comtesse is dressed in a pale-blue satin evening gown, with no other embellishment than the gathers in the fabric. In the isolation and enclosure of the opulent interior, she stands, a pensive silhouette with the perfection of a statue. Her entire torso is reflected and mysteriously reversed in the mirror, which creates a poetic fusion between the real objects and their reflections. The flowers in the Sèvres vases and the red ribbon in her hair give a few lively accents to the fairly chilly and narrow range of grays, blues, and browns.

Théophile Gautier, the impassioned poet and chronicler of the evolution of fashion and the fine arts, greatly admired Ingres's renowned portrait *Baroness James de Rothschild* when he first saw it in the painter's studio, in 1848. This magnificent work, the incarnation of an epoch and a style, is often reproduced in books on fashion history.

Ingres's series of large paintings of prestigious women culminated in 1853 with his *Princess de Broglie*, a portrait of the Comtesse d'Haussonville's sister-in-law. Here, too, we find a strong sense of poise, as well as an even more pronounced taste for the chilly harmonies of blue garments. The curves of the shoulders and of the aristocratic face, with its large sloe-shaped eyes, stand out against the severe rectilinear background, marked with the family's heraldic crest. The effervescence of the fabrics and the sheen of the accessories fill the foreground: a hooped dress with flounced pleats of pale satin, a yellow damask chair upon which the princess is resting her marblelike arms loaded with bracelets, and on which are arranged an Indian shawl, a fan, gloves, and an evening cape, like a luxurious still life.

BUT HIS GREAT OUTING WAS ACCOMPANYING RENÉE
TO THE FAMOUS ESTABLISHMENT OF WORMS [SIC], THE
TAILOR OF GENIUS WHO HAD THE QUEENS OF THE
SECOND EMPIRE BOWING AT HIS FEET . . . THE GREAT
MAN'S SALON WAS VAST AND SQUARE, FURNISHED WITH
LARGE DIVANS. HE WOULD ENTER WITH A RELIGIOUS
AWE . . . THE AIR HAD A WARM FRAGRANCE, AN INCENSE
OF FLESH AND LUXURY THAT TRANSFORMED THE
ROOM INTO A CHAPEL DEDICATED TO SOME SECRET
DIVINITY. OFTEN RENÉE AND MAXIME HAD TO WAIT
IN THE ANTECHAMBER FOR HOURS, IN THE COMPANY
OF TWENTY OR SO FAITHFUL AWAITING THEIR TURN,
DIPPING BISCUITS IN GLASSES OF MADEIRA, SNACKING
AT THE LARGE TABLE IN THE MIDDLE WHERE THERE WERE
ALWAYS BOTTLES AND PLATES OF PETITS FOURS. THESE
WOMEN FELT AT HOME AND TALKED FREELY AMONGST
THEMSELVES.

Émile Zola

The chroniclers of the period, and many writers from Charles Dickens to the Goncourt brothers, have described the immense prestige that was enjoyed by Charles Frederick Worth, the founder of Haute Couture, with its high-society rituals and its parade of publicity. Worth saw himself as an artist—"a composer of fabrics," in his own words—and in a photographic portrait by Félix Nadar, he is shown wearing a velvet cap, a fur-trimmed cape, and a loose cravat in the style of Rembrandt van Rijn and Richard Wagner. Émile Zola's novels describe both the atmosphere of Worth's salons and the evolution of the *grands magasins*, the first French department stores—in other words, the simultaneous development of luxury style for the elite and mass-produced apparel for the general public. Social division was no longer in terms of rank and title, but now in terms of cash.

Charles Frederick Worth was English, and he came to Paris at a very young age. He worked as a professional dressmaker in a small boutique, where he met a lovely sales clerk, who inspired him to create new dress designs (and whom he ultimately married). In the winter of 1857, the House of Worth opened in the Rue de la Paix. Worth soon had such powerful patrons as Princess Pauline von Metternich, wife of the Austrian ambassador, who was no great beauty but quite clever, as her memoirs attest, and extremely chic, as shown in the remarkably modern portrait by Edgar Degas. Through the good offices of the elegant envoy whom he dressed so well, Worth earned the trust of Empress Eugénie, who was very interested in fashion, as well as that of the emperor, because his success had brought about the revival of the silk industry in Lyons and the French textiles industry in general.

With Worth came the beginning of the modern era of fashion. He carried out a sweeping transformation of the traditional clothing industry. He demanded that his profession be granted the privileges and freedoms of a true creative artist, along with the responsibilities and benefits of the head of a professionally run company, which brought together in a single location an array of fields of business that had formerly been separate. Before Worth, tailors and dressmakers had worked out of their homes and remained for the most part unknown. Their clients had given them instructions and brought them the necessary fabrics, which were too expensive for them to purchase in advance. Now the situation was reversed, and when illustrious clients came to Worth, he imperiously presented them with startling new creations he had designed in advance, using fabrics of his own choosing, and which he tailored, after a fitting, to a client's exact measurements.

Worth's other innovation involved the use of live mannequins. His designs were modeled by young women whose physiques matched those of his clients; he called them *sosies*, or doubles. For the reproduction and distribution of his designs, he made use of English-style watercolored prints. Fashion photography came into being after 1880, and Worth's two sons and successors were to make extensive use of it, relying in particular on the services of the firm of Nadar.

Edgar Degas (1834–1917)
Princess Pauline de Metternich, c. 1861.

The famous and brilliantly academic painting of the Empress Eugénie, surrounded by her ladies-in-waiting, by the official court painter Franz Xaver Winterhalter is on permanent display in one of the halls of the Château de Compiègne, where the magnificent Salons d'Automne were held. The empress was at this point not yet being dressed by Worth, but along with her entourage she wears a majestic crinoline, an emblem of the era, which her detractors considered to be ridiculous. Gautier, on the other hand, took up its defense in his essay on fashion: "From this abundance of gathers, which flare out like the skirts of a whirling dervish, the waist emerges slender and elegant; the upper body stands out handsomely; and the entire person forms an attractive pyramid shape."

At the first Impressionist exhibition in the spring of 1874, when the bustle had replaced the bulky crinoline, Pierre-Auguste Renoir presented a ravishing portrait of a young woman he called *The Parisienne*, after the charm of her apparel. The magnificently painted blue dress with its bustle and flounces is reminiscent of the description that Stéphane Mallarmé gave that year of an outfit by Worth: "This garment is as fleeting as our thoughts . . . in the finest of blues, that blue so pale, with a hint of opal, that sometimes envelops the silvery clouds."

Pierre-Auguste Renoir (1841–1919):
The Parisienne, 1874.
Oil on canvas.

John Singer Sargent (1856–1925) *Madame X (Madame Gautreau)*, 1884. Oil on canvas.

Giovanni Boldini (1842–1931) *Madame Charles Max*, 1896. Oil on canvas.

Fashion was no less serious on the other side of the Atlantic Ocean. Comparisons have been made—with particular reference to their psychological insight and the distinctive emphasis that they placed on apparel—between two American-born cosmopolitan observers, the novelist Henry James and the painter John Singer Sargent. Like Whistler and Cassatt, Sargent emigrated to Europe, where he traveled extensively. In 1884 at the Paris Salon, he exhibited the astonishing portrait known as *Madame X*, which caused quite a scandal with its naturalism. Nowadays, we greatly admire its distinctive features, the daring neckline, the stark contrast of the flat silhouette against the neutral background, the shocking power of the color black.

On the other hand, the portrait of Madame Charles Max by the Italian virtuoso Giovanni Boldini is the white-and-gray counterpart to Sargent's portrait in black. It also conveys a general shift in attitude, a transition from a static pose to a spontaneous and animated vision. At the same time, the Austrian painter and decorator Gustav Klimt, skilled in the applied arts, produced a series of ornamental Symbolist portraits, as well as designing numerous articles of clothing for his companion Emilie Flöge. Flöge owned a Haute Couture company in Vienna that was housed in a building designed and constructed by Josef Hoffmann. She did business with French couturiers, in particular Paul Poiret, and later Chanel.

OF ALL THE GOWNS OR DRESSING GOWNS THAT MADAME DE GUERMANTES WORE, THE ONES WHICH SEEMED TO CORRESPOND THE MOST TO A DEFINITE INTENTION, TO BEAR A SPECIAL SIGNIFICANCE, WERE THE ONES DESIGNED BY FORTUNY AFTER OLD DRAWINGS IN VENICE. WAS IT THEIR HISTORICAL CHARACTER, OR WAS IT RATHER THE FACT THAT EACH OF THEM WAS UNIQUE THAT GAVE THEM SUCH A PARTICULAR CHARACTER THAT THE WOMAN WEARING ONE WHILE CONVERSING WITH YOU, OR WAITING FOR YOU, TOOK ON AN EXCEPTIONAL IMPORTANCE, AS IF THIS COSTUME HAD BEEN THE FRUIT OF A LONG DELIBERATION, AND AS IF THIS CONVERSATION WERE DETACHED FROM EVERYDAY LIFE LIKE A SCENE IN A NOVEL?

Marcel Proust

Countess Greffuhle, born Elisabeth de Caraman-Chimay, the cousin of Robert de Montesquiou, was considered as the most perfect beauty of her day. She fascinated Proust and inspired the character of Madame de Guermantes in *Remembrance of Things Past*. In 1893 he observed: "There is no element in her that may be seen in another woman, nor even anywhere else. But the whole mystery of her beauty is in the sparkle, in the enigma of her eyes. I have never seen a more beautiful woman." In this 1896 photograph by Paul Nadar, she wears a black velvet ball gown by Worth decorated with white satin lilies.

Countess Greffuhle,
born Elisabeth de Caraman-Chimay,
in a Worth evening gown, 1896.
Photograph by Paul Nadar.

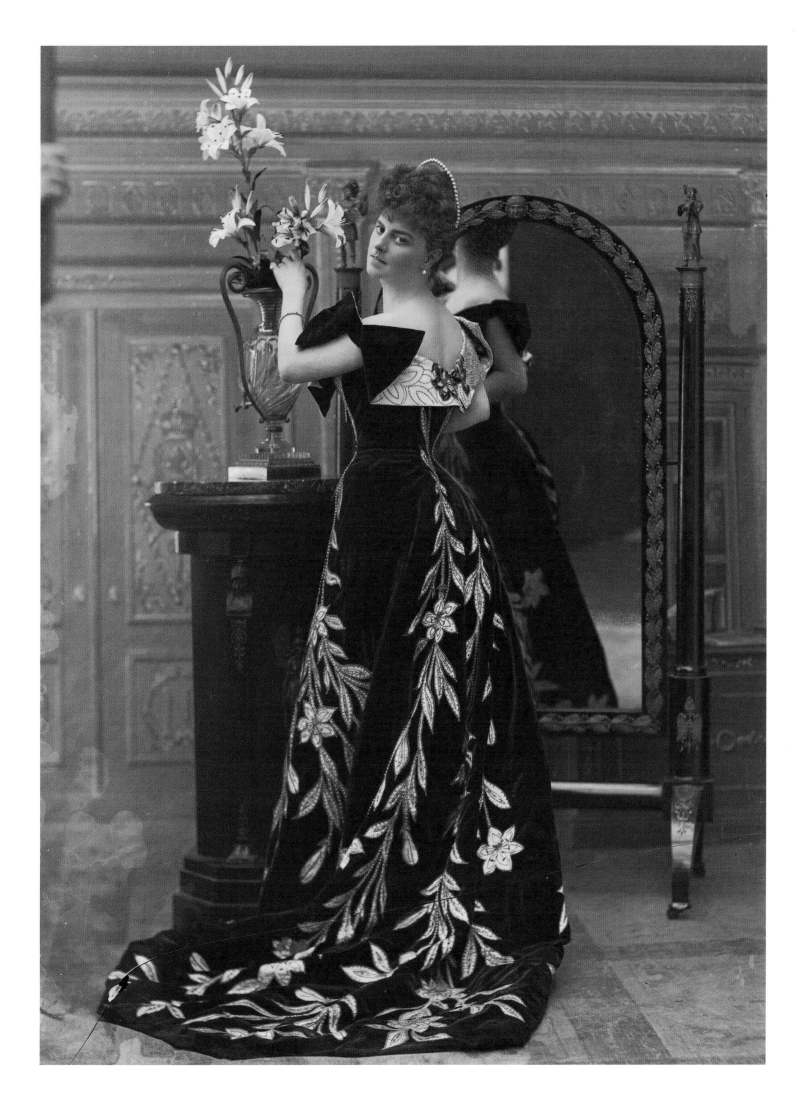

"Dressmaking is an industry whose raison d'être is novelty," declared Poiret, the magnificent, revolutionary turn-of-the-century couturier. After a period of working for Doucet and the House of Worth, traditional fashion houses that were neighbors and rivals in the Rue de la Paix, Poiret went into business for himself in the Rue Auber in 1904, and decided to take a series of bold risks.

He got rid of corsets and freed women's torsos and waists, but shackled their legs with hobble skirts. He revived vertical lines and classical-style tunics, but combined this radical simplification with the love of the vivid colors used by his friends, the Fauvist painters: André Derain, who painted Poiret's portrait; Kees Van Dongen, who captured images of Poiret's fabulous parties; and Raoul Dufy, who designed fabrics for Poiret. His most successful designs were collected in albums by Paul Iribe and Jules Bastien-Lepage and photographed by Edward Steichen. Fascinated by the Orient, Poiret embraced exoticism: harem pants, plumed turbans, and ornamental exuberance.

Paul Poiret (1879–1944)
"Mélodie" Dress, 1912.

Paul Poiret (1879–1944)
"Battick" Coat, 1911.
Photograph by Edward Steichen.

2

OBAZINE AND ROYALLIEU

View of Obazine (Corrèze).

G abrielle Chanel entrusted the writing of her memoirs to one writer after another but no finished text was ever produced, because when it came to her origins, childhood, and youth, no one was able to untangle the truth from her many fabrications. Studies published after her death uncovered her secrets, at least in part. Her ancestors, former landowners turned stablekeepers, came from the poor, deserted hamlet of Ponteils, in the Cévennes Mountains, and from the rural village of Courpière, in the Auvergne, a rough land that forged strong character.

The vicissitudes of the nomadic life of her peddler father resulted in her being born in Saumur on August 19, 1883. She spent her poverty-stricken and chaotic childhood in Issoire, a small town of artisans (for whom she always expressed particular respect), and in Courpière, the tranquil rustic village where her mother was born. She was twelve years old, in Brive, when her mother died, worn out by caring for babies, drudgery, illness, and the escapades of her husband, with whom she had struggled to stay. Chanel's father, silver-tongued and handsome, was constantly on the road; he put his sons on public aid, turned his daughters over to the nearby orphanage, and vanished.

Gabrielle, his favorite child, believed her father's promises and hoped for his miraculous return, and so she denied the ugly truth and idealized his image in order to hide the incurable scars of abandonment. She never admitted the time she spent—a period that was decisive to her future, moreover—living in the Catholic orphanage that occupied the ancient Cistercian abbey of Obazine, in Corrèze, one of the austere wonders of its kind. On its wooded hill between Brive and Tulle, from which vast horizons can be seen, the village clusters around the church with its pointed roofs, octagonal bell tower, and spare proportions, which still possesses its rough-hewn armoire and clear glass windows.

In the adjoining abbey buildings, a magnificent staircase, which fascinated Chanel during the six years she lived here, led from the Romanesque chapter house to the level of the dormitory, whose rooms looked out onto a hallway lined with mosaics featuring mysterious symbols and numbers. In this place of stern and sublime harmony, in a setting of unspoiled nature and pure architecture, the adolescent girl was given a profound sense of aesthetics and a solid preparatory education in housekeeping, the care of linen, and even—a specialty of the institution—the delicate work involved in dressmaking.

It is here that we can find the roots of her tastes and her calling. The strict uniform she wore as a *pensionnaire*, or ward, was in keeping with the bareness of the walls. The white blouse with a black pleated skirt, and a blue suit on Sunday would one day become her fashion emblem. Gaston Bonheur, one of the authors enlisted to help her write her memoirs, noted, without being aware of the existence of Obazine, its influence on her appearance: "She resembled more closely the founder of a religious order than a personality of Parisian life."

Once Chanel came of age, she was freed from her internment, and she spent a period of uncertainty dividing her time between Moulins, where there was a military garrison, and Vichy, a cosmopolitan spa. She held a few jobs—working as a clerk in a hosiery shop, serving water at the mineral springs, and even trying her fortune (without much success) on the vaudeville stage, her body sheathed in the kind of sequined gown that would one day reappear in her fashion collections.

**Inner staircase and pavement,
Abbey of Obazine (Corrèze).**

She dressed herself with an unerring instinct, and her uncommon beauty did not go unnoticed among the well-dressed officers stationed at Moulins. She accepted the courtship of one of them, Étienne Balsan, who was from a prominent family, heir to a sizable fortune, and an enthusiastic horseman. Once his enlistment expired, he took Chanel back to the estate he had purchased and restored in Royallieu, near Compiègne, the finest training facility for his racehorses. Royallieu, where the medieval entry gate still stands, was a venerable monastery founded in 1303 and renovated into perfect seventeenth-century style for the Benedictine nuns, who were expelled after the French Revolution. A portrait of the first abbess, Gabrielle de Laubespine, still hangs on the wall over the magnificent staircase that leads up to the bright and spacious rooms. The handsome windows look out over a spectacular park planted with fine rare plants.

At the age of twenty-five, Chanel discovered luxury and leisure, holidays and sports, the charms of an exquisite and well-run residence—all of which would later serve as inspiration for her own country home in the south of France. A capable rider, she enjoyed long rambles on horseback in the nearby forest. Present yet remote, awaiting a different future, she curiously observed the visits of the high-class dandies and their sensuous mistresses, the actresses and courtesans, emancipated and free-spirited, with their showy outfits, who ruled the world of fashion, which in those days was inseparable from the world of horseracing. Chanel clung stubbornly to her own simple style, bold allure, and intense reserve. Among the women who frequented the cheerful and hospitable (as well as unconventional and nonconformist) home were the famous courtesan Émilienne d'Alençon and the actress Gabrielle Dorziat. One day, they would become customers of Chanel the couturiere, who also counted the singer Marthe Davelli among her models and confidantes.

Gatehouse of the Abbey of Royallieu, near Compiègne.

Émilienne d'Alençon.

Marthe Davelli, Opéra-Comique singer.

CHANEL MODES

Comœdia Illustré, March 1, 1911
Cover by Paul Iribe, hat by Chanel,
worn by the actress Jeanne Dirys.

Soon Gabrielle Chanel had consumed and exhausted the pleasures of the somewhat empty life at Royallieu. In 1909, Balsan offered to put at her disposal his apartment on the Boulevard Malesherbes, in Paris, near the Parc Monceau. There, she began dabbling in what at first seemed like little more than a pastime but soon turned into a business: hatmaking, for which she had an innate sensibility. She bought hat forms in Paris department stores and set about modifying them in a style that was so restrained and pure—clearly a reaction against the reigning style of over-ornamentation—that her female friends were enchanted. They quickly became her customers and brought their social circles with them. Chanel summoned her younger sister, Antoinette, to work as a salesgirl and model. Then Chanel fell in love—it was to be the single great passion of her life—with an English friend of Balsan, Arthur "Boy" Capel. He was extremely attractive, both physically and intellectually; he was a champion polo player, but also an industrial tycoon and a refined man of letters. He reciprocated Chanel's love and taught her to appreciate herself.

"He had a powerful personality, an intense and passionate nature; he shaped me; he knew how to develop in me that which was unique and discard everything else," she said.

With Capel's financial and moral support, Chanel set up a small independent shop in premises at 21 Rue Cambon, and she remained faithful to that street for the rest of her professional life. On the front door, on the mezzanine level, she put up a plaque: *Chanel Modes*.

Thus, she debuted as a milliner at the same time that Jeanne Lanvin entered the field of dressmaking after many years as a hatmaker. The milliners—*modistes*—of Paris that the poet Rainer Maria Rilke described were in those years both numerous and prosperous, for no society lady would dare step out into the street unless she had a different hat to match every outfit and every time of day. Women showed their hair only at dinner or at a ball. The racetrack, the opera, and the theater were ideal venues for the parading of *chapeaux*, both on the stage and in the audience. Chanel's success came so quickly that almost as soon as she set up shop in 1910, illustrated magazines of the time were running full-page depictions, with enthusiastic reviews, of her magnificent creations being worn by renowned actresses. Or, better yet, they would feature her on their covers, with magnificent color illustrations drawn by Paul Iribe, who would one day become her business partner.

In the October 1910 issue of *Comœdia*, Chanel herself was photographed wearing various wide-brimmed hats made of black velvet, with perfect curves—one of them with a tall dark plume, the other with a drooping white feather, setting off wonderfully her delicate profile and the slender elegance of her neck. Headwear had long been the exclusive province of men and a few highborn ladies. Hats came into common use among women—replacing hairnets, veils, and bonnets—at the end of the eighteenth century.

Edgar Degas (1834–1917)
At the Milliner's, 1883. Pastel.

Henri Matisse (1869–1954)
Portrait of Madame Matisse, 1912.
Oil on canvas.

Henri Matisse (1869–1954)
Woman with a Hat, 1905.

After that, the shapes, sizes, materials, and embellishments of hats changed periodically in accordance with trends in hairstyles and fashions in clothing. Édouard Manet, the spontaneous chronicler of Parisian life and its urban poetry, was perhaps the painter who produced, over the course of the years, the most delightful visions of women's hats: hoods with strings, wide-brimmed hats with ribbons, small flowered hats, lace mobcaps, or simple *bibi* caps. He was always happy to accompany his girlfriends Berthe Morisot and Méry Laurent to their milliners, and he would help them select hats before they posed for him.

Beginning in 1880, Edgar Degas produced an astonishing series of images, in oil and pastel, on the distinctive theme of milliners and hatmakers, a theme that was borrowed by many other artists in the years that followed. He showed, from a low-angle point of view, the intimate atmosphere of the millinery shop—its lighting, its furnishings, its displays, the bright colors of the hats on their unusual stands, and the gestures and poses of the clients, who are carefully trying the hats on, cautiously tying the ribbons, gazing at themselves in the mirrors. Nothing could more vividly illustrate the changes that occurred in the shapes of hats and the styles of art over the course of just a few years than Henri Matisse's two famous portraits of his wife, one in 1905, the other in 1912. The first painting caused a sensation and a scandal at the 1905 Salon d'Automne, which marked the historic debut of Fauvism. In that portrait, the explosion of color to which the seated young woman is subjected—her torso in profile, her head turned toward the canvas, her gloved hand on the back of the chair—culminates in the extraordinary multicolored plumage of the hat perched on her brick-red and cobalt-blue hair.

In the second portrait, a work possessing elements of both Cubism and balanced classicism, there is, despite its boldness, a luminous treatment of structure and color, a corresponding simplification of the hat, and a reduction of the facial features to the abstraction of a mask. Later, Matisse himself would design fanciful hats for his models.

Two hats by Chanel, worn by Chanel.
Comœdia Illustré, October 1, 1910.

Hat by Chanel for the actress, Lucienne Roger, as shown
on the first magazine cover to feature Chanel's work.
Cover of *Comœdia Illustré*, September 15, 1910.

COMŒDIA
illustré

Mᴸˡᵉ LUCIENNE ROGER
DANS LE MARIAGE DE Mˡˡᵉ BEULEMANS
LE GRAND SUCCÈS DE LA RENAISSANCE

CHAPEAU, CRÉATION GABRIELLE CHANEL
21, RUE CAMBON.

DEAUVILLE AND BIARRITZ

The Gabrielle Chanel Shop at Deauville, 1913.

Chanel's aunt Adrienne, wearing Chanel, 1913.
Private collection.

D

eauville, a high-society bathing resort and international horseracing venue, was established by the Duc de Morny during the Second French Empire. The town also attracted painters, beginning with Gustave Courbet and the Impressionists, because of the shifting quality of its light—the most beautiful light in all of France, according to Pierre Bonnard. Two buildings were completed at the same time in July 1912, one facing the other—the new casino, built in the style of Versailles's Petit Trianon, and the Hôtel Normandy, in the traditional local style—and these revived the glamour of the resort. The adjoining wings of this immense and pleasant half-timbered hotel, which overlooked the elegant Rue Gontaut-Biron, were also devoted to luxury stores.

In the summer of 1913, an exceptional season, Gabrielle Chanel was on holiday in Deauville with Arthur Capel, who provided the funds and encouraged her to rent a boutique in a good location that enjoyed a great deal of light. On the light-colored awning of her storefront, Chanel inscribed her first and last names in black capital letters. By now her reputation as a milliner was solidly established.

Alongside hats and other easily donned-and-doffed accessories, she soon began featuring attractive and comfortable beachwear and sportswear, which was revolutionary. She also sold overblouses and sweaters to be worn over soft skirts, as well as silk blouses, canvas suits, and lightweight shoes. The Baroness Henri de Rothschild, who had come to a parting of the ways with Poiret, turned to Chanel; others soon followed the baroness's influential lead. The caricaturist known as Sem (Georges Goursat), with his ferocious wit, championed Chanel's cause and helped her business grow by identifying her as the instigator of *le vrai chic*, in contrast with the ridiculous excesses of *le faux chic*.

People came to buy, but they also came to see and admire this intriguing innovator, who had now been joined by her one-time accomplice from Moulins, her young and pretty aunt Adrienne, a heaven-sent fashion model who was an ideal match for her and upon whom Chanel tested her latest creations.

In July 1914, World War I broke out and Deauville, which had been packed, was suddenly empty. The poet Guillaume Apollinaire, sent by *Comœdia* to the "queen of beaches" as an unlikely reporter to cover the social whirl there, abandoned the deserted city—reminiscent of Pompeii, he said—and headlined his article "La fête manqué" (The Party That Wasn't). Chanel held on and stayed where she was. A few weeks later, she found herself dressing both the nurses working in the hotels, which had been transformed into hospitals for wounded soldiers, and the wealthy habituées of the summer resort, caught by surprise by the German advance that was suddenly threatening Paris. The latter had hastened back to their villas, refugees without a suitable summer wardrobe.

Chanel responded to the variety of demands with as much practical aptitude as creative intuition, and her inexorable ascent began: "I had no one working with me but milliners; I transformed them into couturiers. We had no cloth. I cut jerseys for them out of jockey's sweaters, exercise clothes that I wore myself."

Chanel at Biarritz, 1920.
Photograph.

Gabrielle Chanel outside her first shop
in Deauville, with a friend (on her left)
wearing one of her designs, 1913.
Private collection.

Biarritz, on the Basque coast, fashionable ever since the glamorous visits of Empress Eugénie, enjoyed the same cosmopolitan luster as its rival Deauville, but with a dominant Spanish flavor, rather than British. During the war, Biarritz welcomed profiteers and the well-to-do from all over the world. There, far from the line of combat, they enjoyed the pleasures of the ocean and the resort's anachronistic splendors. In the summer of 1915, Boy Capel, who had been recalled to active service, and whose businesses were continuing to hum along profitably, hurried down to Biarritz and its surrounding area for a brief but blissful leave. Chanel, accompanying him, discovered the charms—and the potential profitability—of the area. As her experience and reputation were growing, she seized the opportunity to open not simply an ordinary fashion boutique like the one she had in Deauville, but a full-fledged *maison de couture*, with apparel collections and qualified staff; she retained this shop until the 1930s.

She took up residence in a typical local villa along the road that led down to the beach. At first she rented the villa, but in 1918 she bought it, for cash, having repaid her debts to Capel and established her financial independence.

The neighboring country of Spain had remained out of the fighting and now offered her an aristocratic clientele who knew the resort, which lay within easy reach. The ateliers managed by Chanel's sister, Antoinette, soon employed about sixty people, and an early version of her *robe chemise*, designed in Biarritz, was published in the American magazine *Harper's Bazaar* as early as 1916. After marrying the Russian dancer Olga Khokhlova in Paris on July 12, 1918, Picasso spent his honeymoon in Biarritz, staying at the villa of his Chilean friend Eugénie Errazuriz until the end of September. He drew several portraits in a style similar to that of Ingres, and as a souvenir of his stay, he painted this bold image of bathers, using bright colors and Mannerist-inspired elongated forms.

Pablo Picasso (1881–1973)
The Bathers, Biarritz, summer 1918.
Oil on canvas.

5

THE JERSEY REVOLUTION

Three jersey designs by Chanel.
Les Elégances Parisiennes, May 1916.

In May 1916, *Les Élégances Parisiennes* published illustrations of three Chanel outfits made of jersey, in khaki, white, and dark purple. Jersey, as its name suggests, was originally the heavy knit used for the blue sweaters worn by fishermen in the Channel Islands. Later, the word came to denote a single-knit machine-made fabric with uniform stitches. This material was used chiefly in the production of hosiery, and it was considered impossible to use in dressmaking because of its rough appearance and its open weave. But circumstances—the shortage of textiles, women's demand for practical and serious apparel—led Gabrielle Chanel to use it, and to order the entire stock available from the cloth merchant Jacques Rodier. The use of jersey, which appealed to her memories of a country childhood and challenged every convention of luxury couture, demanded a great purity of line and brought about a revolution in clothing and style.

"When I created jersey," she said, "I freed the body, I abandoned the waistline (which I did not revive until 1930), and I invented a new silhouette. . . . To the great indignation of the other couturiers, I shortened skirts."

Women wearing tailored coats or jackets over shortened skirts—without a waistband, without fitted curves, without ornamentation—acquired an ease of movement and a youthful, svelte appearance, just like Chanel herself, and for the first time in centuries, they showed glimpses of ankle in public, dumbfounding passersby.

Many of those women worked during the war, not only as nurses, but also taking the places of men in public services or in munitions factories. The result of these changing customs and social emancipation was a functional simplification of apparel, a simplification that had already begun with the growing popularity of sports. That social transformation had repercussions on fashion at the same time that Chanel made her debut. "One world was dying, another was coming into existence. I was there, an opportunity beckoned, and I took it. I was the same age as the new century, and so it turned to me for its expression in clothing."

The trend toward simplification also affected the hair. In 1917, Chanel was one of the first to crop short her magnificent head of hair, thus launching a bold style that was soon widely imitated, one that was ideally suited to her kind of beauty. Her Spartan rigor was also applied to furs. With chinchilla from South America and sable from Russia no longer available, she utilized much more modest furs, such as beaver or rabbit, and so turned a shortage into an increase of style and creativity.

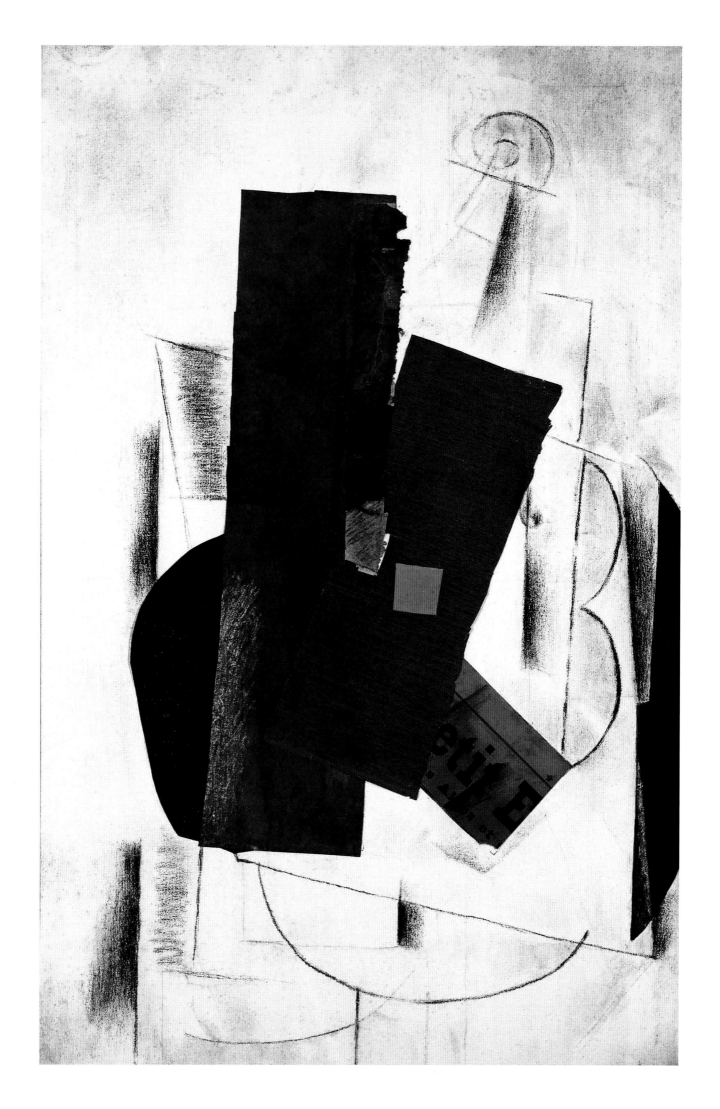

"Teheran" coat by Chanel in beige jersey.
Vogue, New York, February 1, 1917.

Shirtdress by Chanel in beige wool jersey.
Vogue, New York, November 1, 1919.

The actress Cécile Sorel in a striped silk
jersey, by Chanel, designed for Ludovic
Halévy's play *L'Abbé Constantin*.
Vogue, New York, May 1, 1918.

Chanel's use of cheaper fabrics and furs fit perfectly with the Cubist philosophy, which rejected the idea of fine art and instead utilized more humble materials. In September 1912, Georges Braque, who had trained as a housepainter, invented the influential new technique of collage—*papier collé*—as simple in its method as it was infinitely complex in its objectives and results. The monumental collage shown here dates from 1913, the year in which this technique led to the conversion of analytical Cubism into synthetic Cubism, with its rediscovery of color.

A few delicate strokes of charcoal suggest the harmonious shapes of a mandolin and a violin, the musical instruments with which Braque loved to surround himself. Fragments of blue and black paper, newsprint, and woodgrain paper, glued to the surface of the canvas, create a tactile and nonperspectival sense of depth, heightening the two-dimensional plane of space and the subtle interplay of matte colors.

Chanel brought this deceptively simplistic sensibility to her clothing designs. "An evening gown is the easiest thing there is. Now, jersey is quite another matter!" she affirmed, as an expert in the field. Here are three different but successful examples of her skill in using jersey with a narrow range of color dominated by beige, the color that she also established as an element of interior decoration. On the left is a beige jersey coat with navy blue braid, with no trim other than a few tassels. Next is a variant on the ubiquitous *robe chemise*, in beige wool jersey, buttoned up to its open collar, with a broad beaver trim at the bottom of the tunic. On the right is one of the charming outfits worn by Cécile Sorel in *L'Abbé Constantin*, the popular stage adaptation of Ludovic Halévy's best-selling novel. The ensemble is subtle and becoming, in silk jersey with beige and pink stripes.

6

ENCOUNTERS

Pierre Bonnard (1867–1947)
Portrait of Misia Godebska
(detail), 1908–1909.
Oil on canvas.

CHAQUE AUTRE FLEUR NE SAURAIT MÉCONNAÎTRE QUE
MISIA FIT GENTIMENT DE NAÎTRE.

(ALL OTHER FLOWERS CANNOT HELP BUT SEE THAT MISIA
HAS BEEN BORN, AND SO SWEETLY.)

Mallarmé

P aul Morand's diary records the exact date—May 28, 1917—
of the fateful meeting of Misia Sert and Gabrielle Chanel, during a
dinner party at the home of Cécile Sorel. "She impressed me," Misia
recalled, "as someone endowed with immense charm, and as we
were leaving, I complimented her on the very beautiful fur-trimmed
red velvet coat that she was just putting on. She immediately took
it off and placed it around my shoulders, saying as she did so, with
a charming spontaneity, that she was only too happy to make me
a gift of it. Of course, I refused to accept the coat. But it had been
such a lovely gesture that I found her to be absolutely enchanting,
and I couldn't stop thinking about her. The following day, I couldn't
wait to go pay a call on her in the Rue Cambon."

Misia decided to waste no time in introducing her young protégée,
still very inexperienced and shy but nonetheless "irresistible," into
the circles of high society that were off-limits to those who worked
in "trade," and to the enchanted world of artists over which she
reigned with her charm and generosity. She derived her considerable influence from her marriages with Thadée Natanson, editor of
the magazine *La Revue blanche*, and the wealthy publishing magnate
Albert Edwards. Misia was of Polish birth and was a gifted pianist;
she had played for Franz Liszt, Gabriel Fauré, Edvard Grieg, Claude
Debussy, and Maurice Ravel. She had inspired Marcel Proust, who
was a close friend, and had received the praise of such poets as
Mallarmé and Pierre Reverdy. Henri Toulouse-Lautrec, Bonnard,
Édouard Vuillard, Félix Vallotton, and Renoir had painted her portrait
on numerous occasions. The portrait by Bonnard, in 1918, in gray
and pink on a blue background, recalls the styles of Velázquez and
Watteau. Misia's dreamy face and her customary delightful pout only
enhanced her charm. When she discovered Gabrielle Chanel and
transformed her world, Misia was living with the Catalonian painter
and decorator José Maria Sert. She was also devoted to Sergei
Diaghilev and the Ballets Russes, and she frequented the Cubist
circle of painters and poets centered around Picasso.

Gabrielle Chanel, 1909.
Photograph

The actress Cécile Sorel.
Photograph by Reutlinger.

Pierre Bonnard (1867–1947)
Misia Godebska in Profile, c. 1900.

Mlle SOREL

Reutlinger
PARIS

Série 76

PARIS

Boy Capel died in a terrible car crash in December 1919. In order to distract Chanel, who was crippled by grief, Sert and Misia took her on a trip to Italy. The painter proved to be, in her eyes, "an ideal traveling companion—always in a good mood, a tour guide of a prodigious and baroque erudition. He explained everything as I listened, ignorant and attentive; he took pleasure in educating me; he found in me a natural appetite that he preferred to his own immense stock of knowledge." The lessons imparted by the couple soon took root and, in turn, the newcomer wasted no time in charming and delighting their prestigious circle of friends. When Sert left Misia, the tables were turned, and Chanel, at the height of her glory and prosperity, now a hostess and a patron of the arts herself, took Misia under her wing, inviting her along on her luxurious cruises and her delightful tours of Europe and the United States. A passionate friendship would keep these two confidantes and rivals united until the very end. In October 1950, Chanel made Misia's funeral arrangements in the Rue de Rivoli, restoring her friend's living beauty as she lay dressed in white on her canopy bed, covered with white flowers and bedecked in jewelry, a pink satin ribbon on her breast.

In the final analysis, Chanel was forced to admit, "I never had any friend but her. . . . We only love others for their faults: Misia gave me so many and such substantial reasons to love her. Misia was never attracted to anything but the things she could not understand; now she understands nearly everything. As for me, I remained a mystery to her; hence the loyalty that she always denied but which, no matter what, remained constant." What certainly intrigued, impressed, and perplexed Misia, a woman of leisure who was always materially and emotionally dependent, was the freedom that Chanel earned through a combination of her work, her professional success, and her fairytale romances.

COCTEAU TOLD US OF AN AMAZING DINNER PARTY THE DAY BEFORE YESTERDAY AT CÉCILE SOREL'S. PRESENT WERE THE BERTHELOTS, SERT, MISIA, COCO CHANEL, WHO SEEMS TO BE BECOMING SOMEBODY, SIMONE, LALO, BAILBY, FLAMENT, AND HIMSELF.

Paul Morand, May 30, 1917

Portrait of Misia Sert with balloons.
Photographer unknown. Private collection.

PICASSO

"I always felt a solid sense of friendship toward Picasso. I believe that he felt the same way," Chanel said in 1946. In addition to her charm and talent, Picasso respected her down-to-earth qualities—because, as he once said, she had more good sense than any other woman he knew. The period during which they saw a great deal of one another was between 1917 and 1927, when Picasso was actively working on set designs for theater and ballet, from *Parade* to *Mercure* (both by Erik Satie with choreography by Léonide Massine). Picasso and Chanel both had the opportunity during that period to work on two productions directed by Jean Cocteau. Chanel was fascinated and a little terrified by the painter's magnetism, by the burning eyes that turned to stare at the viewer in the self-portraits that he produced during that period. "When he entered a room," she said, "even if I hadn't seen him yet, I could sense that he was there, and that he was looking at me."

The death of Apollinaire, in November 1918, coincided with the Armistice and marked the end of bohemian life for Picasso. He left Montrouge and, after getting married, moved to Rue La Boétie, in the bourgeois art–gallery district. To the amazement of his old friends, he allowed his wife Olga to drag him, however briefly, into the postwar social whirl—not because he liked it, but out of curiosity. Olga bought her clothing from Chanel and maintained a long-term friendship with the couturiere. Picasso, who drew numerous brilliant oil and pastel portraits of Olga in the style of Ingres, also produced a lesser-known red chalk drawing of her, in which she sits in contemplation, looking down, with her hair pulled back. He later gave this drawing to his son, Paulo, as the most intimate and perhaps the most moving image of his mother. During the summer of 1921, he withdrew to Fontainebleau with Olga and Paulo, who had just been born. There he painted immense compositions, both Cubist and classical. When he went alone to Paris, sometimes he stayed at Chanel's townhouse in the Faubourg Saint-Honoré. There she also played hostess to Max Jacob and Reverdy, two poets who had remained penniless and who would tell her about the heroic days of Montmartre and the Bateau-Lavoir.

At the end of May 1917, Chanel watched in astonishment the last performances of *Parade* at the Théâtre du Châtelet. Based on a scenario by Cocteau, Satie's music, Picasso's set designs and costumes, and Massine's choreography flowed together to create the magical fusion of the arts that Apollinaire had described by coining the term "Surrealism." The elaborate series of dances, the magnificence of the production, and the constant need to improve and refine plunged Diaghilev more than once into financial troubles, but he always trusted in luck (or a miracle) to resolve them. Misia, his confidante and supporter, watched over him. In Venice, Chanel listened—without a word, and without doing anything to attract Diaghilev's attention—as he poured out to Misia and other female admirers his desire to restage (if he could only get the financing) Igor Stravinsky's *Rite of Spring*, the infamous production that sparked such a scandal in the spring of 1913. Upon her return to Paris, Chanel sent him, without Misia's knowledge, a sizable and providential check that would allow him to carry out his project; moreover, according to Stravinsky, she offered to make the costumes in her own ateliers. In the blink of an eye, she had completely outclassed, as a patron of the arts, the wealthiest society ladies in the world. Her act of generosity would have remained a secret, had it not been revealed many years later by Boris Kochno, Diaghilev's longtime collaborator.

Once she had been admitted into the intimate circle of this fabulous impresario, who was well aware and appreciative of her generosity and her personality, Chanel closely followed his work and the arc of his life, until the day of his funeral in Venice in 1929, when she and Misia escorted his last remains. "He would duck in to see me," she recalled, "after the ballets, to have a quick bite. . . . [W]ithout removing his white gloves, he'd grab a chocolate. Then he'd succumb to temptation and empty the whole box, his heavy cheeks chomping as he ate, his fat chin—he'd fall ill, he'd spend the night talking. . . . He was the most charming of friends. I loved him for his urgent desire to live, his passions, his ragged clothes—worlds away from the magnificent legend—days without eating, nights spent rehearsing, living in a theater seat, ruining his health and his pocketbook to produce a great show."

Pablo Picasso (1881–1973)
Self-Portrait, 1917. Pencil.

Pablo Picasso (1881–1973)
Portrait of Olga Picasso, 1921.

Overleaf:
Pablo Picasso (1881–1973)
Drop curtain for *Parade*, 1917.

I THOUGHT THAT MANY THINGS WERE PERMITTED TO
YOU . . . BECAUSE YOU WERE NOWHERE A STRANGER,
NOWHERE COULD YOU BE ONE, BEING NOWHERE DEPRIVED
OF A CONNECTION WITH THINGS, WITH LIFE, NOWHERE
SEPARATED FROM BEING, WHICH IS THE GREATEST GIFT OF ALL.

Ramuz

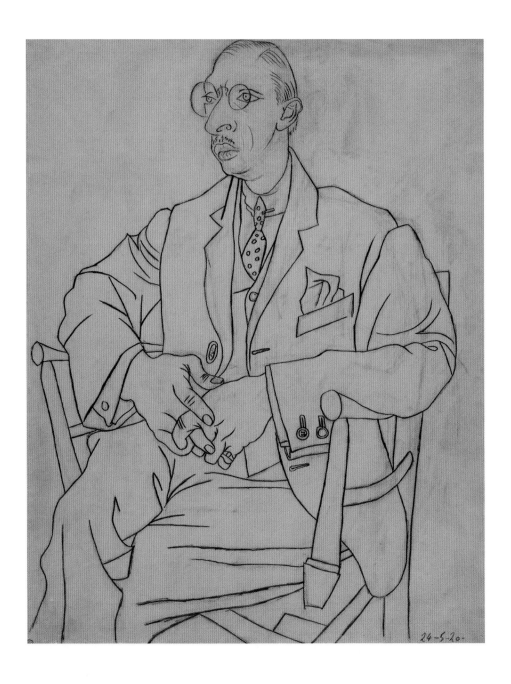

DIAGHILEV AND STRAVINSKY

Chanel's generosity toward Diaghilev extended to his longtime collaborator, Stravinsky, a multitalented genius of the stature of Picasso, with a revolutionary strength and an ability to appropriate the past and make it part of the present. From his safe haven in Switzerland during the war, Stravinsky returned to France in a state of considerable hardship. In the fall of 1920, Chanel lent him her villa at Garches. He lived there for a year with his first wife, Katerina, and his four young children. There he completed his *Concertino for String Quartet* and his *Symphonies of Wind Instruments*, dedicated to the memory of Claude Debussy, and amused himself by creating eight little melodies for piano, which condensed the rhythmic purity of his art into twenty measures. He fell hopelessly in love with Chanel. But instead of joining him in Spain, as he had hoped, she left for Monte Carlo with the young, handsome Russian Grand Duke Dmitri. This unfortunate experience, which very nearly killed Stravinsky, ended up transforming him. She had made a self-effacing, shy man into a tough man with a monocle, the precise opposite of what might have been expected; she had turned a conquered man into a conqueror.

They renewed their bonds of friendship, affectionate and deep. Stravinsky made Chanel a gift of his dearest possession, an icon that he had brought with him from Russia, and she kept it always by her side, on her night table. He had been born a few months before her, and he died the same year she did, in New York. He is buried in the Venice cemetery, near Diaghilev.

There are three portraits of Stravinsky drawn and dated by Picasso. The first of the three, done in 1917 during their trip to Italy for *Parade*, shows torso and face in a frontal view, and was a gift from the painter to the musician. The one dating from December 1920, done during a stay at Garches, showing torso and head in profile, was a gift to Madame Errazuriz, who admired both artists. The largest one, a three-quarter-view portrait that Picasso kept for himself, was done on May 24, 1920, during the production of *Pulcinella*, their jointly created new ballet.

Igor Stravinsky, José-Maria Sert,
Misia Sert, and Gabrielle Chanel
at the Paris Fair, 1920. Photograph.

Pablo Picasso (1881–1973)
Portrait of Igor Stravinsky,
May 24, 1920. Pencil.

Serge de Diaghilev. Photograph.

HENRI BERNSTEIN

One of Chanel's neighbors in Garches was the playwright Henri Bernstein, with whom she was already acquainted. Bernstein was the son of art collectors, and he had been painted at age five by Manet. He was an astonishing individual, a man of culture and vitality, a war hero and a social butterfly who conducted his love affairs with the same brio that he devoted to his successful theatrical productions. Although his star had waned, perhaps inevitably, he was now making a comeback. In September 1919, he took Chanel to meet his friend Liane de Pougy, the dazzling Belle Époque dancer, who later became Princess Ghika, and eventually died as a nun of the Dominican order. In later years, she often turned to Chanel for generous donations to a religious institution for children with birth defects near Grenoble with which she was involved. Chanel visited the institution, in memory of Obazine, and became friends with the mother superior.

In the summer of 1918, while his wife, Antoinette, was in Deauville, Bernstein, with his usual panache, took Chanel to Uriage-les-Bains, where they took the waters together. They both wore the unisex white silk pajamas that Chanel had pioneered as a summer outfit. They were soon joined there by Antoinette and the Bernsteins' young daughter, Georges, who as an adult would marry a painter named Gruber and write a biography of her father. Georges Bernstein Gruber still possesses an interesting collection of correspondence, filled with psychological insights, written to her mother by Chanel, who would always remain, after that brief affair, a close and attentive friend of the couple.

BERNSTEIN HAD HIMSELF ANNOUNCED BY AN ENORMOUS BASKET OF ROSES. HE BROUGHT WITH HIM GABRIELLE CHANEL, THE COUTURIÈRE, A FAIRY BY HER TASTE, A WOMAN BY HER EYES AND VOICE, AND A LITTLE STREET-URCHIN BY HER HAIRSTYLE AND HER SUPPLE AND THIN PHYSIQUE.

Liane de Pougy, September 12, 1919

Gabrielle Chanel with Henri Bernstein and his daughter at Uriage, near Grenoble, 1918. They wear the *pyjama de cure* that inspired Chanel's beach pajamas, the ancestor of the track suit.

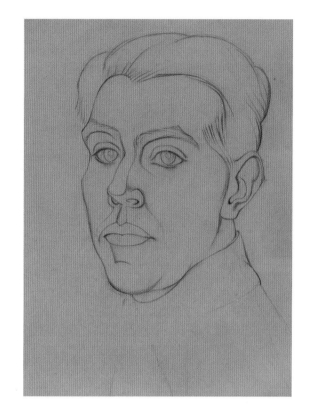

Another great admirer of Chanel was Juan Gris, the youngest and the most rigorous of the four great Cubist painters. In comparison with the Dionysian flair of Picasso, the unrivaled fervor of Braque, and the monumental sincerity of Léger, Gris personified the Apollonian nobility and the elevated lyricism of his birthplace, Castile. In 1916, he had mastered his conceptual vision and moved into a crystalline and architectural phase. From September to November of that year, he lived in Beaulieu, near Loches, in Touraine. This was the birthplace of his wife, Josette. The portrait that he painted of her—one of his masterpieces—is exquisitely feminine in its geometric framework and its solemn orchestration. The harmonious structure of the forms is entirely planar and the range of colors is limited to shades of gray and black, with a little light ocher for the face and dark ocher for the hair. In 1921, he drew a number of pencil portraits in a sparse realistic style, including a self-portrait.

Despite illness, he executed a number of commissions for Diaghilev. Although he kept his distance—either out of discretion or out of stubbornness—from social circles and seldom saw Chanel, she respected him greatly, as a person and as an artist, and she herself tended to practice the same professional austerity. The painter's closest friends—the writer Max Jacob, the poet Reverdy, and the sculptor Jacques Lipchitz—were also in regular contact with Chanel, each in his own way. After Gris's death in 1927, Josette, who had cared for him and supported him during his final illness with an admirable degree of devotion, was forced to look for work. At Picasso's advice, she took a job with Chanel and worked for her for many years, at first in Paris and later in Cannes. At times, she served as an intermediary in the tumultuous relationship between Chanel and Reverdy.

Juan Gris (1887–1927)
Portrait of Josette Gris, 1916. Oil on panel.

Juan Gris (1887–1927)
Self-portrait, 1920–1921.

POETS AND MUSICIANS

Chanel was a friend to poets as well as to musicians and painters. She was visiting Misia when Max Jacob came to call, in the company of a fourteen-year-old prodigy, Raymond Radiguet, with whom Cocteau fell headlong in love. Radiguet died of typhoid at the age of twenty, in December 1923, after writing, in a rigorously classical style, two astonishing novels about his circle and his times. Chanel paid for his hospital bills and his funeral, which she designed all in white—the horses pulling the hearse, the coffin, and the flowers and decorations in church.

Max Jacob kept his profound poetic talents and his mystical aspirations hidden behind the mask of a clown and the flair of a born entertainer. A brotherly companion to the young Picasso, a guide to Poiret in the choice of the most auspicious colors to wear, and an occasional guest of the Princess Ghika at her country home in Brittany, he often visited Chanel to amuse her with his witticisms and his stories, and she often came discreetly to his financial aid.

I STILL REMEMBER A DELIGHTFUL CHRISTMAS PARTY IN THE RUE CAMBON. COCTEAU HAD BROUGHT THE SIX. THE GROUP OF YOUNG COMPOSERS, HEADED BY SATIE, WAS ENJOYING ALL THE EARLY GLORY OF THE BŒUF SUR LE TOIT. POULENC HAD JUST SHED THE UNIFORM. AURIC WAS IN LOVE WITH IRÈNE LAGUT; HONEGGER AND MILHAUD, NOT YET A FATHER, ALREADY HAD A REPUTATION BEHIND THEM, ALTHOUGH MILHAUD WAS NOT YET THE SAINT-SAËNS OF THIS GENERATION. THE RAVISHING AND REFRESHING GERMAINE TAILLEFERRE, JANE BATHORI, RICARDO VINÈS, STRAVINSKY, MORAND, SEGONZAC, SERT, MISIA, GODEBSKI, THE PHILIPPE BERTHELOTS; WE WERE ABOUT THIRTY. FARGUE ARRIVED ANNOUNCING RAVEL; PHILIPPE, WITH HIS CURLS AND FOREHEAD HELD HIGH, THREATENED TO RECITE VICTOR HUGO'S *LÉGENDE DES SIÈCLES*; COCTEAU HAD BROUGHT HIS JAZZ MEN FROM THE GAYA BAR; SEGONZAC DID HIS PEASANT IMITATIONS; HÉLÈNE BERTHELOT HAD A CHINESE SILK GOWN ON THAT RECALLED THE GREEN-ROOM AT THE THÉÂTRE DE L'ŒUVRE. SATIE WAS TELLING ME ABOUT A BALLET. SUDDENLY HE STOPPED TALKING, FOR MISIA WITH HER BRIOCHE ON HER HEAD, ANXIOUS, SMELLING SOME DARK INTRIGUE, WAS DRAWING HER CHAIR CLOSER. SATIE, HIS SPECTACLES ASKEW, SCREENING HIS MOUTH AND GOATEE WITH HIS HAND, MUMBLED TO ME: HERE'S THE CAT, LET'S HIDE OUR BIRDS.

Gabrielle Chanel, in Paul Morand,
The Allure of Chanel

Valentine Hugo (1887–1968)
Portrait of Raymond Radiguet, 1921.

Pablo Picasso (1881-1973)
Portrait of Max Jacob, 1943.

The "Groupe des Six" with Jean Cocteau, 1931.
Left to right: Francis Poulenc, Germaine Tailleferre, Louis Durey. Jean Cocteau, Darius Milhaud, and Arthur Honegger.
In the sketch: Georges Auric.

7

PERFUMES

Lucas Cranach the Elder (1472–1553)
Mary Magdalene, 1525. Oil on panel.

AND PERFUME IS A THING SO VERY MUCH ALIVE THAT IT LIVES AND DIES AS WE DO—DIES AT THE END OF SEVEN YEARS. SO THAT THE WOMAN WHO MADE THE BEST USE OF IT WAS MARY MAGDALENE, FOR WE ARE STILL BREATHING THE FRAGRANCE THAT SHE EXHALED.

Jean Grenier

Until the end of the nineteenth century, prior to the advent of chemical synthesis, all perfumes were derived from animals or plants. Their role in ancient times, especially in the East, was considerable and for the most part ritualistic. Indian Buddhists bathed the statues of their gods with perfumed waters. The ancient Egyptians embalmed their dead, and their priests burned various scents in the temples at appointed hours of the day. In the Bible, the Song of Songs is a hymn to scented herbs, and the sinner who anointed Jesus' feet with a pound of nard, the most costly and precious of perfumes, performed an act of love and purification that saved her soul, even though the disciples considered the expense to have been excessive and wasteful. Mary Magdalene has become the patron saint of perfumers, and her beauty, her extraordinary hair, and her mystical jar of ointment have engendered an extensive iconography. The 1525 painting done by Lucas Cranach the Elder in which Mary Magdalene is depicted in a brocade dress in the midst of an animist landscape corresponds, as we shall later see, to Chanel's tastes in painters of this genre and period.

The ancient Greeks refined the art of cosmetics by adding flower oils to resins, but they looked askance at Asia and its scented luxury. Alexander the Great destroyed Darius III's coffers filled with perfumes and retired to his tent to read the works of Homer. In contrast, ancient Rome, where Nero slept on a bed of roses, was obsessed with perfumes. Incense burners everywhere emitted the intoxicating columns of smoke that gave the word perfume—*per fumum*—its etymological origin. After a few centuries of obscurity, during which the Roman Catholic Church reserved perfumes for purposes of worship, the popularity of perfumes was revived by the spoils of the Crusades, and followed the rise of fashion.

Perfumes based on pure alcohol led to the advent of Hungary water, in around 1380, and later of *eau de cologne*—Cologne water, after the German city—in 1742, which was favored by Napoléon Bonaparte. Each period of history has a perfume of its own, as well as its own distinct style of clothing and furniture. Catherine de' Medici arrived in France with her Florentine perfumers, and Misia claims that it was her own descriptions of Catherine's beauty secrets that first led Chanel toward the realm of perfumes. Major perfume houses were founded in Paris at the end of the eighteenth century. Balzac was a keen student of the language of flowers and Baudelaire took a nostalgic and poetic view of perfume. Perfume lost its religious associations and became instead an aesthetic concern. The publication of the novel *À rebours* (Against the Grain) by Joris-Karl Huysmans in 1884 coincided with a shift in the world of perfume. The book's protagonist, Duc Jean des Esseintes, rejects nature and, cloistered in his bedroom, sets himself to learn the "syntax of odors," and even contrives to compose a number of "aromatic stanzas." And that is precisely what master perfumers managed to do, by combining in their laboratories the synthetic products of modern organic chemistry and highly concentrated flower extracts, essences that were obtained in factories at Grasse through the use of volatile industrial solvents. Jean-François Houbigant introduced *Fougère Royale* (1882) containing coumarin, the House of Guerlain produced *Jicky* (1889) with vanillin, and L.T. Piver crafted *Trèfle Incarnat* (1900) with amyl salicylate; these early synthetic perfumes were created through a process of abstraction analogous to that being used in contemporary art. In 1911, Poiret had made the pioneering move of linking haute couture and perfume production, but what he produced, under the trade name of Parfums de Rosine—named after his daughter, Rosine—were still old-fashioned blends, and not innovative fragrances.

Bottle of Chanel No. 5 perfume, as launched in 1921. Photograph by Daniel Jouanneau.

Pablo Picasso (1881–1973) *Bottle and Wine Glass on Table*, 1912.

Chanel burst onto the scene at the perfect moment, with the same verve she had shown in her debut in the world of fashion, the same daring and flair. City-dwellers' sense of smell had atrophied over the years, but Chanel, like her close friend Colette, had preserved and refined her country-girl's sensitivity to fragrance. She claimed that she could distinguish the scent of the forest of Compiègne from a single branch, and if offered a bouquet of flowers, she could detect the odor of the hands that had gathered them. It was almost certainly during her Mediterranean affair with the Grand Duke Dmitri that she made the acquaintance of Ernest Beaux in his factory in La Bocca. Beaux was an exceptional perfumer who had begun his career in Russia, where he was born.

Like any successful artistic creation, perfume is the result of both technique and inspiration. Beaux was attempting to work with aldehydes, powerful but unstable synthetic substances that were not yet being utilized in perfumes. His objective was to re-create—with a combination of eighty ingredients—the unique sensation he had experienced while north of the Arctic Circle, as he inhaled the intensely fresh scent of rivers and lakes under the midnight sun. Chanel encouraged him to pursue his experiments and dared him to try extreme solutions in his search for the strongest and the subtlest accents. Beaux received a welcome visit from the enthusiastic caricaturist Sem, who would eventually design the poster for the perfume that was still in development. In 1921, Beaux submitted to Chanel two lists of samples, numbered from 1 to 5 and from 20 to 24. She selected sample 22, which she released several months later, and sample 5, which she chose to launch alongside her collection on the fifth of May (the fifth month, of course). Five was her lucky number, a positive symbol with multiple meanings, the *quintessence* (fifth essence) of Paracelsus and his fellow alchemists. This scent was the foundation of all the true designer perfumes that would follow, the first of the influential series of floral aldehydes. Chanel's revolutionary perfume, No. 5, the success of which continues to this day,

is legendary around the world, and it can be considered a personal and independent creation—not just a scent for one's handkerchief, but rather an aroma for the entire body and its freedom and beauty.

Each era has its own way of storing perfumes. Receptacles of wood or ivory and vases of polychromatic glass were among the wonders of Egyptian art. Rome had its rhinoceros horns, the Renaissance its pomanders, the eighteenth century its vermeil coffers, the Romantics their medallions. From 1880 on, ornamental glass and crystal containers by René Lalique ruled supreme. Chanel imposed a strict and imperious sense of style on the bottle for her perfume, a clear glass square with sharp corners, allowing the golden liquid within to be seen, the stopper marked with her initials, the white label with its black lettering bearing her surname and the triumphant numeral 5. In 1924, the brothers Pierre and Paul Wertheimer founded the Société des Parfums Chanel, with Ernest Beaux as director of production and chief perfumer. He created many other prominent perfumes of different types for Chanel, with names that reflected their scents: *Gardénia* (1925), *Bois des îles* (Wood of the Islands, 1926), *Cuir de Russie* (Russian Leather, 1927). In 1970, shortly before her death, Chanel, who liked to cite Paul Valéry's bon mot "A woman who does not use perfume has no future," presented her last perfume, No. 19, named after the day of her birth, a splendid floral harmony with woody notes.

Henri Laurens (1885–1954)
Bottle and Glass, 1919.

Chanel perfumes: Gardenia
(1925), Bois des îles (1926),
Cuir de Russie (1927).

8

EMBROIDERY

Detail of coat from the Chanel Haute
Couture collection, Fall–Winter 1922.
Black crepe with colorful Russian-inspired
point de Beauvais embroidery by Kitmir.

There are two chief methods of embellishing clothing, sometimes used in combination: embroidery, which is applied directly to a fabric, and lace, with its open pattern of threads. Liturgical embroidery, which came out of Byzantium, is one of the great arts of the Middle Ages. Clothing embroidered with silver and gold threads and beads and precious stones reached its apex in Europe during the sixteenth and seventeenth centuries, as an emblem of luxury and social prestige.

Sumptuary laws were passed to limit its use, and this led to a rise in the popularity of lace, at first attached to the collar and cuffs, and later extended to the bodice and the front of the skirt in the eighteenth century. The bourgeoisie of the nineteenth century displayed their wealth with the use of expensive handmade lace and white-thread embroidery. Multicolored embroidery and the use of precious materials were revived at the turn of the twentieth century, with Far Eastern and Slavic influences. Embroidery is one of the jewels of Russian folk art, with types that vary by region. Peasant dresses, shirts, and blouses all feature magnificent embroidered decorations with intense colors and traditional motifs—geometric, symbolic, and floral. Upon their arrival in Paris in 1909, the Ballets Russes astonished the city with their folk costumes. In 1912, Poiret brought back from his trip to Russia a number of embroidered tablecloths that he used as inspiration for his exotic outfits.

The Callot sisters specialized in lace, and Jeanne Lanvin specialized in embroidery. The popularity of embroidery was widespread in the years following World War I. Chanel was all the more willing to go along with this fashion because her villa in Garches, where she lived for an idyllic period with her Grand Duke Dmitri, was a veritable Russian colony. In her expanded premises at 31 Rue Cambon, she hired Prince Koutousof as her *chef de reception*, along with a number of women from Russia's exiled high society. In 1921, she set up an embroidery studio under the supervision of Dmitri's sister, Maria Pavlovna. On May 15, 1922, *Vogue* magazine observed: "No one knows how to adorn apparel with original embroidery better than Chanel." Without renouncing the purity of her line and her basic tones of black and brown, she decorated her crepe dresses with colorful embroidery, her velvet coats with crystal beads. She borrowed motifs from Asian fabrics, but most of all from Russian folk art.

Actresses played an important part in the success of couturiers. Henri Bernstein's best-known play was *The Secret*, first produced in 1913 and often revived before becoming part of the repertoire of the Comédie Française in 1933. In March 1919 it was staged at the Théâtre du Gymnase, and one of the actresses, Véra Sergine, wore a costume by Chanel, a charcoal-gray crepe georgette dress with pink net, adorned with embroidery in a Chinese motif. The skirt and the sleeves were edged with moleskin.

Coat from the Chanel Haute Couture collection, Fall–Winter 1922. Black crepe with colorful Russian-inspired point de Beauvais embroidery by Kitmir.

Gabrielle Réjane, who was closely allied at the beginning of her career with the couturier Jacques Doucet, was also a great friend of Misia, whom she tried to enlist in her theater troupe. In 1922, her son Jacques's wife, Anne-Marie, was photographed frequently in fashion magazines, dressed in creations by Chanel. Here she is shown with her hair shingled, in front of an oriental screen. Her pink crepe evening gown is embroidered with crystal beads.

Véra Sergine in Henry Bernstein's play
The Secret, wearing a Chanel dress.
Femina, Paris, April 1, 1919.

Madame Jacques Porel wearing a Chanel
dress. *Vogue*, Paris, September 1, 1922.

9

ANTIGONE AND LE TRAIN BLEU

Antigone brought by two guards before Creon.
Greek vase painting from Lucania, c. 380–370 BCE

Guard: **IT IS NOW FOR YOU TO DO AS YOU WILL, KING. TAKE THE GIRL, JUDGE HER, AND CONFOUND HER. AS FOR ME, I AM FREE, I HAVE BEEN CLEARED OF ALL SUSPICION.**
Creon: **YOU HAVE BROUGHT HER TO ME; BUT WHERE DID YOU CAPTURE HER, AND HOW?**
Guard: **SHE WAS BURYING THE CORPSE. YOU KNOW THE WHOLE STORY.** (*Creon turns to Antigone.*)
Creon: **AND YOU, WHO STAND THERE WITH LOWERED HEAD, DO YOU CONFESS OR DENY THE DEED?**
ANTIGONE: **I CONFESS; I WOULD NOT THINK OF DENYING IT.**
Creon (*to the Guard*): **YOU MAY TAKE YOUR LEAVE, YOU ARE FREE OF A GREAT BURDEN.** (*The Guard leaves. To Antigone.*) **AND NOW, ANSWER ME STRAIGHT, WITHOUT ANY SPEECHES. DID YOU KNOW OF THE INTERDICTION THAT I HAD DECREED?**
Antigone: **YES, I KNEW OF IT: HOW COULD I IGNORE IT? IT WAS TOO CLEAR.**
Creon: **AND YOU DARED TO VIOLATE IT?**

Antigone: **YES, BECAUSE IT WAS NOT PROCLAIMED BY ZEUS! NOR BY JUSTICE ENTHRONED BESIDE THE INFERNAL GODS; THOSE ARE NOT THE LAWS THAT THEY LAID DOWN FOR MAN, AND I DID NOT THINK THAT YOUR STRICTURES WERE POWERFUL ENOUGH TO PERMIT MORTALS TO TRANSGRESS OTHER LAWS, THE UNWRITTEN, UNSHAKEABLE LAWS OF THE GODS! THESE WERE LAID DOWN NEITHER TODAY NOR YESTERDAY, NONE CAN SAY WHEN THEY WERE MADE.**
COULD I VIOLATE THEM OUT OF FEAR OF YOU OR ANYONE, AND EXPOSE MYSELF TO THE VENGEANCE OF THE GODS? DID I NOT KNOW THAT THIS WOULD MEAN MY DEATH? EVEN IF THERE HAD BEEN NO INTERDICTION. BUT FOR ME TO DIE BEFORE MY TIME, HEAR ME LOUD AND CLEAR, IS A GOOD THING; FOR ONE WHO LIVES AS I DO, SURROUNDED BY WOES WITHOUT END, HOW COULD DEATH NOT BE A GOOD THING?
TO BE PUT TO DEATH IS NO CAUSE OF SUFFERING FOR ME. BUT IT WOULD HAVE BEEN ONE IF I HAD LET THE BODY OF ONE OF MY MOTHER'S SONS BE DENIED A TOMB AFTER HIS DEATH. YES, THAT WOULD HAVE CAUSED ME TO SUFFER; I DO NOT SUFFER FROM THIS. I MAY SEEM TO BE ACTING LIKE A MADWOMAN. BUT THE ONE WHO TAKES ME FOR A MADWOMAN MAY WELL BE A MADMAN.
…
Creon: **EVEN DEAD, AN ENEMY IS NEVER A FRIEND.**
Antigone: **I AM ON THE SIDE OF THOSE WHO LOVE, NOT HATE.**

Sophocles, *Antigone*

Jean Cocteau was present at the home of Cécile Sorel when Misia and Chanel first met in May 1917. He was already a friend of Misia, and he soon became a friend of Chanel as well. The crisis brought about by World War I triggered a return to Mediterranean art forms and classical sources. Cocteau joined this movement, encouraged by Satie, who had composed a work for voice and small orchestra entitled *Socrate*, and by Radiguet, who was enamored of classical purity.

In the summer of 1922, during Cocteau's productive stay with Radiguet at the Lavandou, he wrote *Plain-Chant*, his finest collection of poems, as well as two short novels and a free adaptation of Sophocles's masterpiece, *Antigone*, a play with universal resonance. Cocteau produced a modern "abridgement" of *Antigone* into a one-act play, comparing his version to "an ink sketch based on a canvas by an Old Master," or "a photograph of the Acropolis taken from an airplane."

Arthur Honegger, the lone Swiss member of the group of composers called Les Six, later composed a magnificent opera based upon the same source material, but limited his score for Cocteau's adaptation to musical accompaniment by harp and oboe.

Picasso, who was in his classical phase, designed the black shields of the guards (after motifs taken from Greek vases) and the clusters of masks of the women, old men, and children who made up the chorus. The blue backdrop was evocative of the sunny day on which the tragedy takes place. A panel of white wood was hung beneath the masks, and left blank for decoration. Picasso showed up at the last moment and transformed the wood into marble with a blood-red scumble, and with a few strokes of ink, he made Doric columns spring magnificently into being.

Cocteau asked Chanel to design the costumes, "because she is the greatest couturiere of our age, and it is impossible to imagine the daughters of Oedipus poorly dressed," as he told the press. Chanel, who had recently acquired a Greek marble statue to display in her drawing room and who had just presented a collection that featured some items evocative of classical drapery, rose to the challenge brilliantly. Her reconstructions of period costume—made of heavy wool in a neutral color that fit perfectly with the stage design—were greeted with acclaim and shown in a number of magazines.

Charles Dullin in the role of Creon, in Jean Cocteau's *Antigone*, wearing a jeweled headband created by Chanel, 1922.

Chanel costumes for Jean Cocteau's *Antigone*:
Antigone and Ismène.
Vogue, Paris, February 1, 1923.

The premiere took place on December 20, 1922, at the Théâtre de l'Atelier in Montmartre. The theater had been taken over a few months earlier by Charles Dullin as a workshop for daring theatrical experimentation with new actors and an innovative repertoire. The performance of *Antigone* was preceded by a curtain-raiser by Luigi Pirandello, *Il Piacere dell'Onestà* (The Pleasure of Honesty).

Dullin had been acquainted with Picasso since his arrival in Paris, and he had first met Chanel in 1911, when she was secretly taking classes in rhythmic dance in the Rue Lamarck from the dancer Élisabeth Toulemont (known as Caryathis), who was living with Dullin at the time. Ancient Greek depictions of the myth of Antigone are quite rare, so it is interesting to compare photographs of the stage design with the illustration on the Lucanian vase in the British Museum.

Dullin played the tyrant Creon, a cruel guardian of the city's laws—laws that Antigone transgresses for the sake of the higher values of conscience and love. On Dullin's forehead was a metallic headband in which glittered paste gems, probably the first piece of costume jewelry designed by Chanel.

The role of the blind prophet Tiresias—whose harsh rebukes Creon ignores in a bitter dispute—was played to the verge of hysteria by the poet Antonin Artaud, a regular actor in the troupe and an impassioned supporter of the theater company in his writings. Artaud's Greek girlfriend, Genica Athanasiou, played a deeply moving Antigone, with her eyes circled in black, a pure and aristocratic face, white makeup and close-cropped hair. She was dressed in a white-and-brown woolen gown that was knotted with cords, and from time to time she draped herself in a solemn mantle in order to amplify her gestures—a mantle that her sister, Ismène, does not wear. "Antigone has decided to act," Cocteau explains. "She wears a magnificent cape. Ismène is not going to act. She wears everyday clothing."

The words of the Greek chorus, considerably condensed from the original text, were spoken by Cocteau himself, through a megaphone concealed behind a grille built into his mask. Chanel's reputation was already so great at this point that the French press praised the costumes more than the play, although Ezra Pound spoke highly of the production in the American magazine *The Dial*.

WHILE THE PITOËFFS WERE PLAYING AT THE FOOT OF
MONTMARTRE, DULLIN WAS ORGANIZING THE THÉÂTRE
DE L'ATELIER HIGHER UP NEAR THE SACRÉ-CŒUR. IT
WAS THERE THAT HE PRESENTED MARCEL ACHARD'S
ADAPTATION OF *THE BIRDS* BY ARISTOPHANES, WITH
MUSIC BY GEORGES AURIC AND SETS DESIGNED BY
JEAN HUGO. IT WAS ALSO THERE THAT IN SILENCE AND
GREATLY MOVED WE SAT THROUGH COCTEAU'S *ANTIGONE*,
FOR WHICH PICASSO HAD DESIGNED THE SETS: A GREAT
BLUE SKY, WHITE STEPS, WHITE COLUMNS, AND MASKS.
ATHANASIOU PLAYED THE PART OF ANTIGONE, AND
HER GREEK ACCENT, WHICH GAVE THE FRENCH WORDS
AN UNACCUSTOMED SONORITY, MADE HER AUSTERE
LINES STRIKE EVEN MORE DEEPLY INTO OUR HEARTS.
HER FACE WAS MADE UP INTO A WHITE MASK, AND IT
WAS AS IF SOPHOCLES' REBELLIOUS, MAJESTIC, CRUEL
BUT RIGHTEOUS MAIDEN HAD RISEN FROM HER AGE-
OLD TOMB TO UTTER THE LIMPID WORDS OF HER GREEK
TRUTH RESURRECTED BY A FRENCH POET FOR US IN THE
CONFUSION OF OUR PARISIAN METROPOLIS. SOPHOCLES
MAY NOT HAVE NEEDED COCTEAU TO BE UNDERSTOOD,
BUT WE NEEDED COCTEAU TO DISCOVER SOPHOCLES.
THE ATELIER THEATRE WAS TOO SMALL TO SATISFY ITS
DIRECTOR FOR LONG. HE TOOK HIS MARVELOUS STAGE
SENSE ELSEWHERE, WHILE COPEAU'S VIEUX COLOMBIER
THEATRE WAS CONVERTED INTO A MOVIE HOUSE.

Maurice Sachs

Born a year before his friend Cocteau, Paul Morand, a perceptive chronicler of his time, debuted with a collection of poems and short stories, with a preface by Proust. In 1924, he published his first novel, *Lewis and Irène*, a depiction of the business world with a narrative based on Chanel and Boy Capel's affair. Morand's book *The Allure of Chanel* remains an engrossing account of the couturiere's life, which Morand followed with interest to the very end.

Radiguet's posthumous novel, *Le Bal du Comte d'Orgel*, was also published in 1924. The book was based on the parties and receptions given by Count Étienne de Beaumont, elegant society host and a rival of Diaghilev, in his mansion in the Rue Masseran. Sert and the artist Marie Laurencin were often involved in creating the décor for those parties. In June 1924, following the production of the ballet *Mercure*, Picasso appeared at one party dressed as a toreador, flanked by his wife, Olga, and Eugenia Errazuriz wearing costumes that may well have been designed by Chanel. Amazing photographs of these society balls, and of the cosmopolitan milieu of Paris, were taken by the American artist Man Ray.

ON SEPTEMBER 26, 1923, THE COLLECTOR AND ART DEALER RENÉ GIMPEL NOTED IN HIS *JOURNAL*: "I AM GOING TO SEE MARIE LAURENCIN, WHO IS WORKING ON THE SETS AND COSTUMES FOR THE RUSSIAN BALLET *LES BICHES* . . . SHE EARNS MONEY DOING PORTRAITS, BUT SAYS THAT NOW SHE WANTS TO PAINT ONLY GULLS, THAT IS, HER FRIENDS, THOSE FOOLISH ENOUGH TO SEE A LIKENESS WHERE THERE IS NONE. SHE HAS JUST DONE CHANEL'S PORTRAIT AT HER REQUEST, BUT THE COUTURIÈRE REFUSED TO TAKE IT. 'AND YET,' MARIE SAID, 'I PAY FOR THE DRESSES I ORDER FROM HER . . . SHE WANTS ME TO START ANOTHER PICTURE, BUT SHE SHAN'T HAVE IT; I AM GOING TO PRETTIFY HERS AND SELL IT.'"

Marie Laurencin (1885–1956)
Portrait of Gabrielle Chanel, 1923. Oil on canvas.

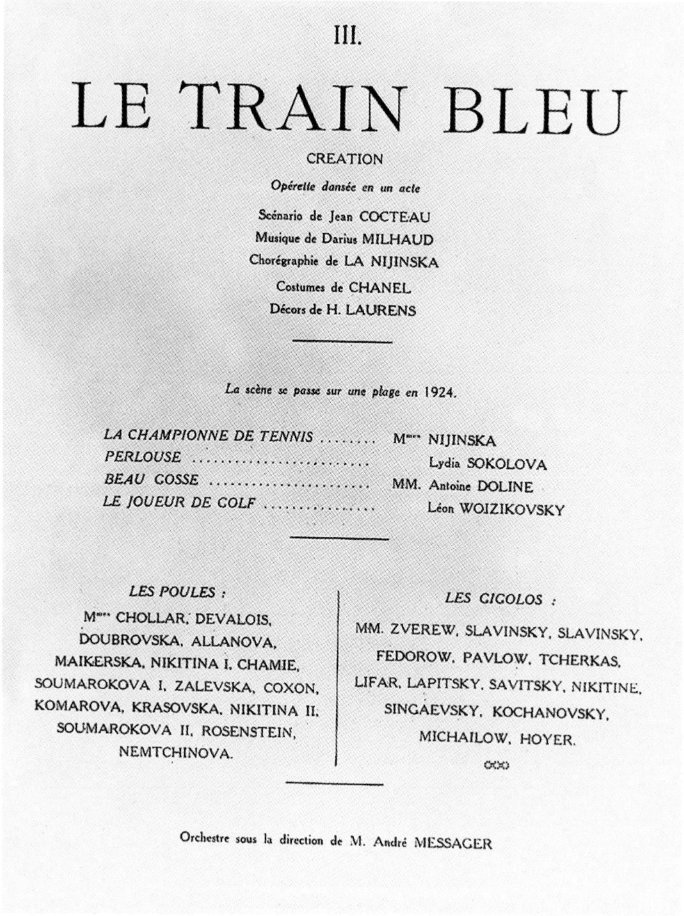

Chanel was thus able to finally make her way into the fabulous world of the theater, about which she had been dreaming since she was a girl, and she moved on from theater to dance, from Dullin to Diaghilev. First performed on June 20, 1924, at the Théâtre des Champs-Élysées, *Le Train Bleu* was not really a ballet at all, but more of a choreographed musical comedy—an *opérette dansée*, according to the wording on the program designed by Picasso at the behest of Boris Kochno.

Picasso was also the artist behind the monumental stage curtain, created by enlarging a painting in gouache on wood created during the summer of 1922. The giant female figures of Picasso's classical period were generally motionless, self-contained in the fullness of their forms. But the two women who are shown here running freely along the beachfront, arms outstretched and breasts bouncing, seem to be drawing Heaven and Earth toward them with their cosmic impetus. Diaghilev was overjoyed with the curtain, and its appearance was greeted with a fanfare by Georges Auric. Picasso signed the curtain, dedicating it to Diaghilev.

"Le Train Bleu" was the name of the luxury express train that carried aristocratic passengers from Paris to the Côte d'Azur. Cocteau's ballet, a mocking celebration of new social mores, is a study of flirtatious games played on the beach and the new mania for sports. The *Beau Gosse* (Handsome Hunk), a role that was played with brio by the English dancer Anton Dolin in an athlete's jersey with his hair slicked back, impressed the gigolos and the *poules* (chicks) with his acrobatic prowess.

Program for the ballet *Le Train Bleu*, 1924.

Pablo Picasso (1881–1973)
Two Women Running on the Beach, summer 1922.
Gouache on wood.

Page 106:
Jean Cocteau with Lydia Sokolova, Anton Dolin,
Léon Woïzikovsky, and Bronislava Nijinska in *Le Train Bleu*.
Page 107: Lydia Sokolova as Perlouse and Anton Dolin
as Beau Gosse (The Handsome Hunk), 1924.

The Golfer, of Polish birth, mimicked the sartorial elegance of Edward, Prince of Wales, in action on the green, while the Tennis Champion had the daring outfits and the bandana-style headband of the real-life tennis champion Suzanne Lenglen, the idol of the public and the darling of the photographers. This role was played by Vaslav Nijinsky's sister, Bronislava Nijinska, who was also in charge of the choreography. Nijinska remained faithful to the Russian tradition of stylization, and she soon clashed with Cocteau, who demanded scenes of pantomime and acrobatic fantasies; Diaghilev acted as mediator. Chanel was in her element making athletic outfits in jersey, since she wore them herself and had introduced them to the broader public.

What caused widespread consternation, however, was the choice of Darius Milhaud, a fairly serious composer who usually worked on themes from the Bible, to compose a score of light, cheerful music. Equally surprising was the choice, for set designer, of the Cubist sculptor Henri Laurens, who had never been to the beach in his life and who never dabbled in the social world.

Laurens was a friend of Braque and Gris, as well as Amedeo Modigliani, who painted his portrait twice; he also illustrated the works of Reverdy and Radiguet, and he would later create the marvelous sculptures *Les Ondines* (The Water Sprites) and *Les Sirènes* (The Mermaids). Laurens came out with his head high, designing droll renderings of beach cabins in the geometric style of his collages and constructions. During rehearsals, Chanel noticed in the group of dancers a young refugee from Kiev with a superb body and considerable gifts. She pointed out this promising youth to Diaghilev, and in time he became Diaghilev's protégé: Serge Lifar.

LE TRAIN BLEU **WAS AN OPERETTA WITHOUT WORDS. IN ASKING ME TO COMPOSE THE SCORE FOR THIS LIGHT, GAY, FRIVOLOUS, OFFENBACHIAN SUBJECT BY COCTEAU, DIAGHILEV KNEW THAT I COULD NOT INDULGE IN THE KIND OF MUSIC WHICH I WAS USED TO AND WHICH HE DID NOT LIKE. THE STORY TOOK PLACE IN A FASHIONABLE VACATION RESORT TO WHICH THE ELEGANT BLUE TRAIN EACH DAY BROUGHT ITS LOAD OF BEACHGOERS; THEY MOVED ABOUT ON THE STAGE PRACTICING THEIR FAVORITE SPORTS: TENNIS, GOLF, ETC. ANTON DOLIN WAS ABLE TO GIVE FREE REIN TO HIS ACROBATICS AND CHOREOGRAPHIC FANTASIES.**

Darius Milhaud

Amedeo Modigliani (1884–1920)
Portrait of Henri Laurens, 1915.

Serge Lifar, 1925. Photograph.

10

ELEGANCE AND SIMPLICITY

Madame Varda in a Chanel evening
gown of white georgette crepe.
Photograph by Edward Steichen.
Vogue, New York, October 1, 1924.

E ach and every trend is formed in a reaction to the preceding one. "I wonder why I ventured into this profession," Chanel said, "and why I was seen as a revolutionary in the field. It was not really to create what I liked as much as it was to remove from fashion, first and foremost, the things I did not like. . . . I was the tool of Destiny in a necessary process of cleansing." We have already mentioned some of the factors that led to this purification of fashion, comparable to the process undertaken in the aesthetic realm by Cubism and its offshoots.

World War I modified social structures and triggered the emancipation of women, freeing them to engage in an active life and loosening the moral strictures that bound them, allowing them to participate in sports and exercise as well as the kind of frenzied dancing that was typical of the Roaring Twenties. For those women and that time, Chanel invented an appropriate style of dress that could be donned and fastened without external help. "Paris is a feast," Hemingway exclaimed. Parisian haute couture, where women were the dominant force—Jeanne Paquin, Jeanne Lanvin, Madeleine Vionnet, Gabrielle Chanel—recruited its clientele from among the wealthy and cosmopolitan class drawn to the pleasures of the French capital, then in the midst of an artistic and social boom.

After a brief pause, fashion soon established a new type of woman, the *garçonne* (the tomboy)—this was also the title of a scandalous and very popular novel written by Victor Margueritte in 1922—who had a slender and androgynous silhouette, with short-cropped hair beneath a cloche hat. Flat surfaces and straight lines replaced the gathered and rounded curves that were associated with the female figure, while plain white and black overtook the exotic medley of hues that Poiret had tried to bring back into vogue after his trip to Morocco.

As his success dwindled, Poiret accused Chanel of having brought the world "*le misérabilisme de luxe*" (luxurious poverty) but the more refined sensibility that she had brought to fashion was more appropriately described by Balzac's phrase "*le luxe de la simplicité*" (the luxury of simplicity).

Photography and film boosted the appeal of black and white clothing, allowing its simple and autonomous shapes to be perceived at a glance. In 1923, Edward Steichen, former assistant to Alfred Stieglitz and an impassioned follower of contemporary art, replaced Adolphe de Meyer as the fashion photographer for American *Vogue*, which had been publishing a French edition since 1920. He had already done some test photography for Poiret in 1911 that complied with the established pictorial conventions of the time. Now, however, he abandoned the romantic and hazy style of his predecessor in favor of a straight, objective approach, with no props or manipulation.

Marion Morehouse in a bright blue crepe evening dress with shaded fringe by Chanel. Photograph by Edward Steichen. *Vogue*, New York, November 1, 1926.

Chanel suit of plain and printed crepella.
Vogue, Paris, April 1, 1925.

Chanel evening gown in white georgette crepe.
Vogue, Paris, April 1, 1925.

The elegant and svelte model stands against a plain and geometric background. The sharp, bold lighting emphasizes the architectural perfection of the dress on the model's poised body—the rectangular blouse that shows off the slim neck, the loose ribbon around the low waistline, the slanting pleats of the asymmetric skirt.

In 1925, the immense Exposition Internationale des Arts Décoratifs et Industriels Modernes (International Exhibition of Modern Industrial and Decorative Arts) in Paris brought the new trends of geometric design and the ornamental revivals of the modern style together in an eclectic blend. The Purist pavilion was designed by the architect Le Corbusier; within it, Fernand Léger displayed his wall paintings. The *Revue Nègre* made its triumphant debut that same year in the Champs-Elysées music hall, with Josephine Baker and the jazz musician Sidney Bechet. Both of these events had significant repercussions in the world of fashion.

The most significant development of the year, however, was the short skirt, anathema to religious authorities around the world and actually outlawed in a number of American states. Chanel, for aesthetic reasons, never took the skirt above the knee. The sustained simplicity of the silhouette was enlivened by embroidery in curved or triangular patterns, and floating panels at the sides. She used a great deal of wool crepe, for both dresses and overcoats with turned-down collars and turned-up sleeves.

Steichen's favorite model was Marion Morehouse, whom he found distinctly feminine without any complacent sentimentality. Later, she married the American poet E. E. Cummings, whom she had met in Paris. In 1926 she wore a bright blue crepe Chanel dress with a shimmering silk fringe. Fringes were one of Madeleine Vionnet's specialties, and often adorned her bias cut fabrics.

The dancing girl picking flowers is a wall painting from the villa of Stabiae. As she turns her back to the viewer, the supple grace of her step and her undulating garments is revealed. The rear view, a favorite technique of the painter Watteau and revived frequently by the finest fashion photographers, shows off the form and beauty of a costume that seems poised to fall.

In her book, *Inventive Paris Clothes 1909–1939*, with magnificent photography by Irving Penn, Diana Vreeland featured the three-piece Chanel outfit pictured here—a sleeveless top, a straight skirt, and a cardigan vest, all covered with black sequins—and added this appreciative comment: "This evening dress has enjoyed the honor of multiple imitations since its was first created. And it remains eternally perfect."

"Primavera": wall painting
from Stabiae (Bay of Naples).
First century BCE.

Chanel sequined suit, 1926.
Photograph by Irving Penn.

IN OUR DAY A WORK OF ART SHOULD BE
ABLE TO STAND COMPARISON WITH ANY
MANUFACTURED OBJECT.

Fernand Léger

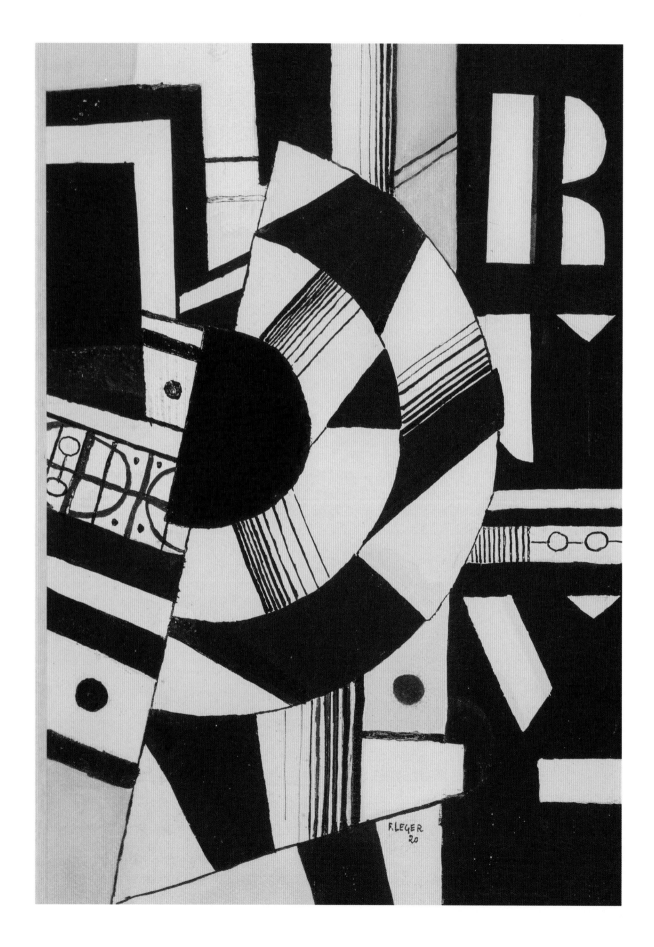

Technology was marching onward as well. The automotive industry began in France, but for years it exclusively served a luxury clientele and their individual preferences. By standardizing components and introducing the assembly line, Henry Ford established mass production in the United States, with a single type of car, painted in black. When *Vogue* published Chanel's little black dress in 1926 as the new uniform of the modern woman, it was immediately compared to Ford's democratic Model T car. The fine pleats and folds running across the dress, converging in a quadruple pleat at the waist, were the only evidence of the flawless rigor of its geometric structure.

After it first appeared at the court of the duchy of Burgundy in the fifteenth century, the color black was conveyed to Catholic Spain and to the Protestant Netherlands, and went on to assume varied symbolic functions throughout the history of clothing. During the nineteenth century it was the dominant color of men's garments. Chanel introduced black into women's clothing as an antidote to the garish colors that shocked her, as well as for its uncompromising nature. Her close-fitting black dress was as functional as an automobile, and the impeccable purity of its cut echoed the artistic style of Léger in his mechanical period. The painter did not imitate machines; rather, he integrated them into his works through signs and symbols.

Fernand Léger (1881–1955)
Composition, 1920.

Ford car, 1925 model.

Black Chanel dress.
Vogue, Paris, November 1926.

Ina Claire, a close follower of Chanel, was the first actress to dress as naturally for the stage or screen as for the street. Her sparkling dress of black tulle and silvery beads has a deep plunging neckline at the back, forming an oval shape whose lines harmonize perfectly with the curve of her shoulders and arms. "The front never moves," said Chanel, "it's the back that does the work. A big woman always has a narrow back, a slender woman always has a broad back. . . . The entire articulation of the body is in the back; all the gestures begin from the back."

The short sleeveless bolero jacket, which Chanel regularly used in her daytime outfits, also serves as a brilliant accompaniment to her evening wear, especially when enhanced with sequins, as it is here. The dress in black Roman crepe is adorned with a double fringe embroidered with jet, with asymmetrical panels.

Ina Claire in a black and silver Chanel gown, in embroidered tulle with beads and sequins. Photograph by Edward Steichen. *Vogue*, New York, May 1, 1926.

Marion Morehouse in a black crepe Chanel gown with an overskirt of fringe embroidered with sequins. Photograph by Edward Steichen. *Vogue*, New York, May 1, 1926.

11

ORPHÉE

Jean Cocteau, 1926.
Photograph.

An affectionate camaraderie as well as a working relationship linked Chanel and Cocteau throughout the years between the World Wars. The couturiere often invited the poet to stay as a guest in her apartment in Paris or her Mediterranean villa. She also helped him financially during the challenging periods of his illness and cures for drug addiction. "A biography of Cocteau is not necessarily a biography of Gabrielle Chanel," said Cocteau's biographer, Francis Steegmuller, "but there are points at which you could substitute one for the other, or else follow both of their parallel paths. That is the case when Chanel made costumes for one of Cocteau's plays, with the repercussions that they had on fashion, as was the case in particular with *Train Bleu* and *Orphée*." To overcome the despair that engulfed him after the death of Radiguet, Cocteau sank into opium use and turned briefly to religion. In Villefranch-sur-Mer in September 1925, he completed his play *Orphée*. Soon afterward, he read it to Stravinsky, his neighbor in the Nice area. His experiences with drugs and religion and his obsession with his dead young friend all permeated his contemporary version of the ancient myth, whose plot he preserved intact. Virgil and Ovid both told the legend of the Thracian poet who descended to the underworld and attempted, in vain, to bring back his wife, Eurydice, and who charmed animals, trees, and rocks with his sighs of grief.

That story has been a source of inspiration to many musicians and painters. Apollinaire and Rilke both identified the song of Orpheus with the very life breath of poetry. Cocteau followed in their footsteps, but the dramatic action of his play demanded a number of new elements: the character of Heurtebise, the angelic glazier whose power over mirrors gives access to the Kingdom of Shadows, and the figure of Death as a "very pretty young woman" dressed in a ball gown beneath a surgeon's smock. A clairvoyant horse, which takes the place of the more traditional ouija board, added an unexpected element of spiritualism and farce and disconcerted critics.

The first production of the play took place on June 15, 1926, at the Théâtre des Arts, with the marvelous actors Georges and Ludmilla Pitoëff as Orpheus and Eurydice. The key role of Heurtebise, which Cocteau himself performed when the play was revived the following summer, was first played by Marcel Herrand. Chanel created the simple yet elegant costumes, in keeping with her style, and Jean Hugo, a gifted painter and theater designer and a familiar figure in society milieux and artistic circles, designed the sets. The two bewitching film versions of the same story that the obsessed Cocteau made in 1950 and 1960 have since overshadowed the memory of the original play, though it was crucial to the poet's artistic development.

Pablo Picasso (1881–1973)
Portrait of Jean Cocteau, 1917.

WE MUST USE THE COSTUMES OF THE PERIOD IN WHICH
THE TRAGEDY IS PERFORMED. ORPHEUS AND EURYDICE
WEAR COUNTRY CLOTHES, THE SIMPLEST POSSIBLE, AND
THE LEAST VISIBLE. HEURTEBISE HAS THE BLUE OVERALLS
OF A WORKER, A DARK SCARF AROUND HIS NECK, AND
WHITE CANVAS SHOES. HE IS SUN-TANNED AND BARE-
HEADED. HE NEVER LEAVES HIS GLASS-CUTTING MACHINE.
THE COMMISSIONER AND THE BAILIFF WEAR BLACK
TUNICS, PANAMAS, GOATEES, AND BUTTON BOOTS.
DEATH IS A VERY BEAUTIFUL YOUNG WOMAN IN A BRIGHT
PINK BALL-GOWN AND FUR COAT. HER HAIRSTYLE, GOWN,
SHOES, MANNERISMS, AND BEARING ARE IN THE LATEST
FASHION. SHE HAS A MASK WITH LARGE BLUE EYES
PAINTED ON IT. SHE SPEAKS RAPIDLY, WITH A SHARP AND
ABSENTMINDED VOICE. HER NURSE'S BLOUSE MUST ALSO
BE THE VERY EPITOME OF ELEGANCE. HER ASSISTANTS
WEAR THE UNIFORM, GAUZE MASKS, AND RUBBER GLOVES
OF SURGEONS.

Jean Cocteau

IN JUNE, REHEARSALS BEGAN IN THE PITOËFFS' THEATER.
TO MAKE THE WINGS OF THE ANGEL HEURTEBISE
("CLASH-WIND"), WE BOUGHT THE TOOLS OF AN
ITINERANT GLASS-CUTTER WE RAN INTO ON THE
BOULEVARD DES BATIGNOLLES.
THE WHITE HORSE THAT SPOKE BY STRIKING THE
GROUND WITH HIS HOOF, THE DIABOLICAL AND
SURREALISTIC HORSE, WAS SUPPOSED TO OCCUPY THE
CENTER OF THE STAGE AND ATTRACT THE ATTENTION
OF THE AUDIENCE. HIS HEAD SEEMED RATHER TOO
SMALL. ON THE WAY TO THE BAZAR DE L'HÔTEL DE VILLE
DEPARTMENT STORE TO GET THE OILCLOTH THAT WE
WERE GOING TO USE TO REPRESENT THE MIRROR, THE
DOOR TO THE INVISIBLE WORLD, COCTEAU AND I WERE
CAUGHT IN A TRAFFIC JAM NEAR THE CENTRAL MARKET.
THERE, FRAMED BY THE WINDOW OF THE CAB, WE SAW
THE WHITE HEAD OF A DRAY HORSE APPEAR. COCTEAU
SAID TO ME, "LOOK HOW BIG THE HEAD OF A HORSE
IS!" IN MY DEFENSE, I BORROWED FROM THE PICCO BAR
IN THE RUE WASHINGTON A PLASTER HORSE USED TO
ADVERTISE A BRAND OF WHISKEY WHOSE HEAD HAD THE
SAME PROPORTIONS AS THAT OF MY CARDBOARD HORSE.
THIS DID NOT CONVINCE THE AUTHOR OF *ORPHÉE*. SINCE
IT WAS TOO LATE TO MAKE ANOTHER HORSE'S HEAD,
WE PUT TWO LITTLE SHUTTERS LIKE THE ONES OFTEN
SEEN IN BARS IN FRONT OF THE HORSE'S CHEST, AND SO
MASKED THE DISPROPORTION BETWEEN THE HEAD AND
THE LEGS.

Jean Hugo

Jean Hugo (1894–1984)
Sets for Jean Cocteau's play *Orphée*.
L'An Vivant, Paris, August 1, 1926.

12

VARIATIONS AND CURVES

Inside Chanel's boutique, 31 Rue Cambon, Paris.
Model wearing a gown from the 1927 collection.
Photograph by Adolphe de Meyer.
Harper's Bazaar, New York, April 1927.

After moving from *Vogue* to its rival magazine, *Harper's Bazaar*, Adolphe de Meyer maintained the shimmering and painterly style of photography, with its skillful backlighting effects, that had brought him such great success. In the spring of 1927, he placed his model in an asymmetrical black Chanel dress on the famous staircase of Chanel's new offices in the Rue Cambon, whose pure and sober modernism set a trend in the industry. The glass bowl lamps hanging from the ceiling spread an even light and the crystal flowers are reflected by the mirrored walls, opening up and enlarging the space. That year saw the peak of short, straight dresses with low waistlines, which Chanel had mastered by varying the cut of the fabric and the interplay of the floating panels or crisscrossed bands against the solid-color surfaces. She was roundly acclaimed for the skill of her creations, but also for the things she wisely chose to reject. "[S]he possesses to the highest degree," *Vogue* acknowledged, "the art of avoiding mistakes."

The reproductions that follow illustrate the evolution of Chanel designs over three years, from the shortest tubular style to the revival of long gowns with volume and width. In 1928, the waistline has risen back toward its natural position; a black sheath with narrow straps has a low-cut bodice that fits closely down to the slender hips, and then flares downward in asymmetrical skirts, longer in back than in front. In 1929, a dress in wild-rose crepe has spiraling flounces that extend and drape to form a short train at the back, while a light scarf floats like a small cape.

In 1929, economic crisis struck the United States and then spread, the following year, around the world. Interestingly enough, this was when the long and luxurious skirt came back into fashion, along with the genuine fur coat. Colette, who was hostile to flat, rectangular fashion, was overjoyed. "It came, inevitable and logical," she wrote, "so romantic that it brings a tear to your eye, so feminine that it ravishes you, fragile as a happy dream, it came, the reaction of 1930." Chanel brought back organdy, finished with beadwork, and her apricot-colored dress fits closely at the natural waistline, then spreads out to the floor in an elegant halo.

Chanel gown in black taffeta.
Vogue, Paris, May 1928.

Chanel gown in rose georgette crepe.
Vogue, Paris, September 1929.

The photographer George Hoyningen-Huene, the son of a Baltic baron, began to work at *Vogue* in Paris in 1925. He was influenced by Steichen, and he developed a personal style with an innate sense of elegance and a respect for clothing as an expression of culture. He earned Chanel's confidence and friendship, and he admired her classicism, a style he favored in his own work.

He demanded from his models a sense of "inner calm" and the sculptural beauty of poses inspired by the Greeks. When he went to Greece on an aesthetic pilgrimage for the first time in 1931, he was so overwhelmed by the experience that he was unable to take a single photograph. He was particularly skilled in using light to enhance the texture of fabrics and the intensity of folds and pleats. The painting *Judith* by Giorgione was long thought to be by Raphael, and during the eighteenth century it was in the Crozat collection in France. It was later purchased by Catherine the Great of Russia. Judith is depicted placing her bare foot on the severed head of Holofernes and unveiling, beneath her parted tunic, the splendid flesh of her leg, a weapon every bit as redoubtable as her sword. Over time, erogenous zones have often varied, and by the time Marlene Dietrich first appeared on screen, the focus of physical desire was chiefly on a woman's legs.

The photographer Irving Penn composed a dazzling vision of a blue silk tulle Chanel dress with sequins. There are some uncanny resemblances to the painting by Giorgione: the placement of the jewelry around the neck, the suggestive baring of the leg, similar gestures of the hands, and the exquisite cuff bracelet.

Chanel gown in apricot organdy with beadwork.
Vogue, New York, April 12, 1930.

Chanel dress with long back, in blue tulle
with sequins, 1927–1928.
Photograph by Irving Penn.

Woman with Ermine, attributed to El Greco, is generally thought to be a portrait of his enigmatic wife. This painting made a strong impression on the young Baudelaire when it was displayed at the Louvre with Louis-Philippe's Spanish collection, long before the genius of the master from Toledo had been rediscovered. The dramatic lighting accentuates the face and the hand between the pale fur and the dark background. This mysterious figure, with its large eyes, is without doubt one of the most unusual and bewitching images of feminine beauty.

After 1930, fur once again became an essential component of an elegant woman's wardrobe, as well as a marker of her social class. In 1931, the American actress Ina Claire chose a Chanel suit of black wool trimmed with red fox for her last film, *The Royal Family of Broadway*.

Ina Claire in a black Chanel suit
trimmed with red fox.
Photograph by Von Horn.
Vogue, Paris, January 1931.

Attributed to El Greco (1541–1614):
Woman with Ermine, 1577–1578.
Oil on canvas.

Chanel evening gown in spring-green chiffon.
Photograph by Hoyningen-Huene.
Vogue, New York, February 15, 1931.

Saint Modeste, north portal of Chartres Cathedral,
13th century.

Chanel was not unaware of the profound connections between art and fashion, but she scorned couturiers who fancied themselves artists. "I insist that couture is a technique, a profession, a form of commerce. . . . That clothing might attempt to rise to the level of beauty of a statue or emphasize the qualities of a sublime heroine is wonderful, but that would never justify a couturier in . . . claiming to be, or posing as, [or] expecting to become an artist."

In 1931, Hoyningen-Huene reached the apex of his style. His model, dressed in a spring-green chiffon outfit, is a study in sculptural beauty: the subtle curve of the neckline, the long flowing sleeves with elegant folds, the graceful belt, the delicate headband encircling the hair (evocative of the Middle Ages, which art historians of the period were studying with intense interest). Proust fell under the spell of the Middle Ages and hoped to construct his masterpiece, he said, like a dress and like a cathedral. Saint Modeste, on her pillar in the north porch at Chartres, is a sublime image of the noblest and most appealing modesty. Gothic statuary invented its own pure expression of the feminine ideal by harking back to the Greek sources which, as we have seen, so captivated all the creative artists who surrounded Chanel.

FOR THE WORLD, GREECE IS STILL THE PENSIVE ATHENA LEANING ON HER SPEAR. NEVER BEFORE HAD ART UNITED SPEAR AND THOUGHT.

André Malraux

The pensive Athena at the Acropolis Museum—who gazes, leaning on her spear, at the stele of her sanctuary—embodies the absolute union of thought and feeling. This is a masterpiece of severe classicism in which maximum emotion is expressed through minimum resources. The warrior goddess is also counselor to Ulysses and protectress of the arts and of the glorious city that bears her name, as well as patron goddess of the spinners and the weavers who made the *peplos* in which she is dressed.

"Women think of all colors," Chanel remarked, "but not of the absence of color. I've said that black contains everything. So does white. They both possess an absolute beauty. It's a perfect form of harmony. Dress women in black or white at a ball: you notice only them."

Lady Iya Abdy, an extremely attractive Russian-born actress and society lady, is shown wearing a white chiffon dress by Chanel, with whom she was very close. She has the same radiance as Matisse's *Woman with a Madras Hat,* painted two years earlier in solid white on a red-and-green background.

Lady Abdy in a white chiffon
evening gown by Chanel.
Vogue, New York, April 1931.

Henri Matisse (1869–1954)
Woman with a Madras Hat, 1929.
Oil on canvas.

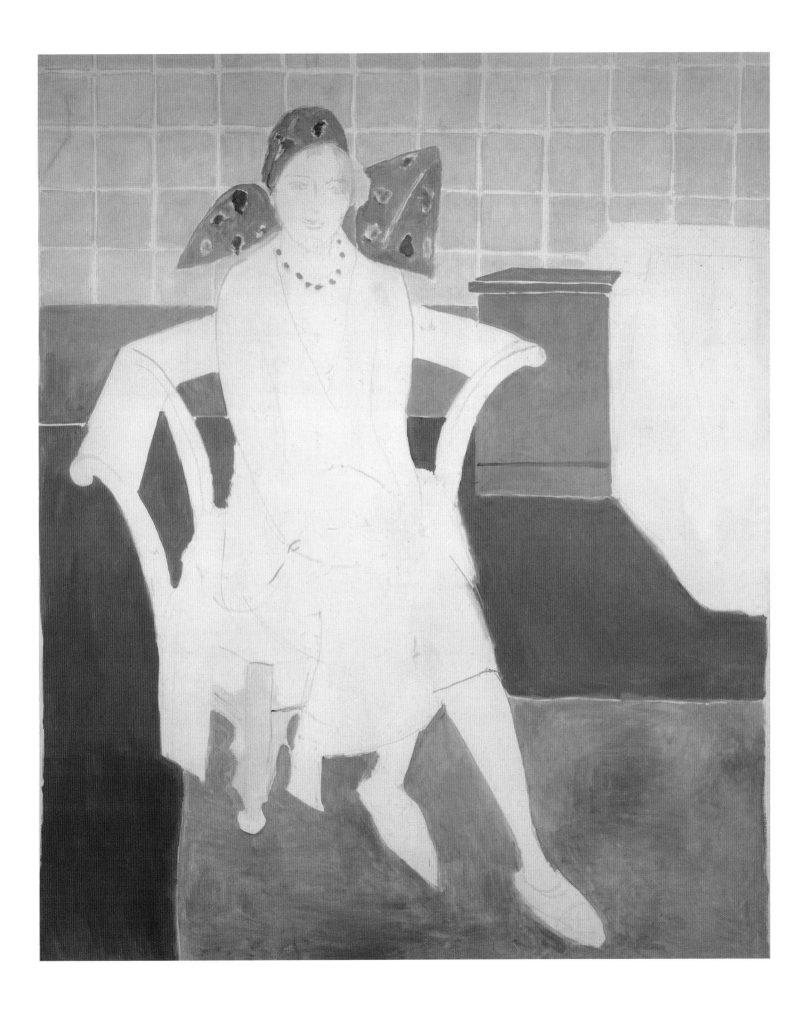

13

LONDON

Chanel in London, 1931.
Photograph.

Great Britain, the homeland of elegant menswear, sent her finest designers of women's clothing to Paris. Among them were Charles Frederick Worth, the father of haute couture; John Redfern, the inventor of the tailored suit for women; and Edward Molyneux, whose *maison* opened for business in 1919, with restraint and quality as its hallmarks. In London, the preeminent fashion designer was Norman Hartnell, who opened his business in 1923 and later became dressmaker to the royal family. Chanel was introduced by Étienne Balsan to "the turf," the Anglophile world of horseracing. The society types she encountered at Royallieu all used English perfumes made by Penhaligon's.

Boy Capel reinforced her love of British life and British ways. He commissioned an English tailor to produce more elegant versions of the simple outfits that she had made with her own hands, and "all of Rue Cambon," she later said, "came from that decision." Fond of novels, she devoured English literature, and she identified with Cathy, the indomitable heroine of Emily Brontë's *Wuthering Heights*. At Deauville, a substantial number of her clients were English, and the metamorphosis of fashion took place via British-style sweaters and jerseys.

After her Slavic interlude with the handsome Dmitri, who led her briefly toward embroidered Russian clothing, her affair with the Duke of Westminster, between 1924 and 1930, brought her back into the English ambiance. Their meeting took place at Christmas in Monaco, and the introduction was made by Vera Bate Lombardi, an English friend of Chanel's who was well connected in London high society and a fine ambassador, along with Daisy Fellowes, for Chanel's creations. The "urchin look" suited their Anglo-American type. The Duke, a cousin of the King and a close acquaintance of both Winston Churchill and the Prince of Wales, was also the wealthiest man in England. Chanel was mistrustful at first, but in time she came to see that such great wealth, in combination with such excellent manners—simple and considerate—effectively erases all sense of vulgarity and is transformed into magic.

The duke was genuinely enamored, and she felt secure and relaxed in this dreamlike world. She accompanied him on cruises on both of his yachts—one for the Mediterranean Sea, the other for the Atlantic Ocean—and she spent time with him in his many homes, always kept ready for occupation: in Normandy, on the Scottish moors, in Norway (where they went salmon fishing), and in his stately home at Eaton Hall, near Chester. This immense ancestral home had been rebuilt at the turn of the nineteenth century in a dizzying composite style, but life within the mansion was an endless party, with resident musicians and all the necessary domestic comforts. The surrounding parklands offered all the enchantments of the English countryside, tastefully cultivated.

When Chanel returned to Paris, the duke's special couriers brought her his messages along with meadow flowers picked at dawn or baskets full of delicacies, at the bottom of which there sometimes glistened a fabulous piece of jewelry. She rejected his offer of marriage and broke off the relationship without looking back; pleasures that come too easily eventually dull the senses, and her overriding passion remained her demanding profession, a feeling she shared with the writers and artists whose stimulating presence she had missed while in England.

Her business connections in London thrived, however, and she drew numerous ideas for her designs from her stays on that side of the Channel: striped waistcoats inspired by the livery of the footmen at Eaton Hall, sailors' caps that she adapted and adorned with jewelry, a profusion of jackets with a masculine cut, sports coats, tailored suits for the races, and Scottish tweeds. "I import my tweeds from Scotland—homespuns have replaced crepes and muslins. I make sure that my wool isn't washed much, so that it's softer. In France, they wash it too much."

In May 1932, in the Grosvenor Square apartments lent to her by the Duke of Westminster and redecorated in keeping with her own tastes, she organized a charity fashion show featuring 130 outfits, all made with British fabrics and presented by amateur models.

The *Daily Mail* of May 14, 1932, reported on the success of the event: "She attracted five to six hundred people every day and dressmakers from all over the globe attended. Many of the women who attended brought their own dressmakers because, given that the collection would not be for sale, Mademoiselle Chanel had authorized the visitors to copy what they saw." Among the society ladies who attended the fashion show was Lady Pamela Smith, photographed both seated and in profile by Adolphe de Meyer, against a specially chosen floral backdrop. She wore a pink lace evening gown and an ostrich-feather boa of the same color.

Lady Pamela Smith in an evening gown
of pale pink lace with an ostrich boa.
Photograph by Adolphe de Meyer.
Harper's Bazaar, New York, June 1932.

14

HOLLYWOOD

Gloria Swanson dressed by Chanel
in the film *Tonight or Never*, 1931.

ANNA DE NOAILLES
COLETTE

"The Americans," Chanel once said, "have invited me a hundred times to go and launch my fashion in California. I turned down the offer because I knew that the result would be artificial, and therefore negative." All the same, she accepted an invitation to Hollywood, though the trip proved to be brief. During the summer of 1930 in Monte Carlo, Dmitri introduced her to Samuel Goldwyn, American film industry tycoon, who controlled the largest movie production and distribution networks. He offered her a dazzling contract to dress, twice a year, the constellation of starlets making movies for his studio. In an effort to beat the Great Depression, he wanted to boost the usual reasons to pay to see his movies by adding the prestige of fashion and the celebrity of a couturiere who had herself become a star. To his astonishment, Chanel hesitated for many months before agreeing to undertake the journey.

She finally made up her mind to go in April 1931. She took as her traveling companion Misia, whom Sert had by this time left for a young Georgian beauty, Isabelle Roussadana "Roussy" Mdivani, whose brothers were living in California. In New York, Goldwyn arranged for Chanel and Misia to board a sumptuous white train. At the Los Angeles station, Chanel was welcomed by Greta Garbo. "Two Queens Meet" went the newspaper headlines. The legendary city of film laid out all its spectacular charm and luxury in her honor, but Chanel, accustomed to true luxury and great creative minds, was quick to perceive the artifice and the childish excess behind that sparkling surface. She made friends with Marlene Dietrich and Greta Garbo, and they remained close. At times they were also her clients. The only personality that truly made an impression on her was Erich von Stroheim, the actor and director, who was a brilliant and sardonic interpreter of the craziness of Hollywood.

Chanel was already experienced in designing costumes for theater and ballet. She observed great movie costume designers at work, experts such as Mitchell Leisen and Gilbert Adrian, who, under the supervision of Cecil B. DeMille, worked to create stylized and even exaggerated fashion. Black-and-white movies demanded clothes that looked sensational. But Chanel could not tolerate the constraints of this kind of work, nor was she willing to put up with the whims of stars who would not accept a single design, however perfect it might be. The parting of the ways was inevitable and the American press spiritedly took Chanel's side. Nevertheless, Chanel ventured to work with Gloria Swanson, a dazzling star then at the height of her glory and fame; what is more, she had a sense of fashion. Later, Swanson designed clothing for herself and for the fashion industry.

Chanel was contracted to design the costumes for Swanson's movie *Tonight or Never*, based on a Broadway play. The movie premiered in December 1931. Fittings were done twice in Paris, before and after the summer vacation, but Swanson was pregnant and had gained weight in the interim. As she recalls in her autobiography, *Swanson on Swanson*: "The following day Coco Chanel, tiny and fierce, approaching fifty, wearing a hat, as she always did at work, glared furiously at me when I had trouble squeezing into one of the gowns she had measured me for six weeks earlier. It was black satin to the floor, cut on the bias, a great work of art in the eyes of both of us."

Edouard Vuillard (1868–1940)
Portrait of Countess Anna de Noailles, c. 1932.
Charcoal on canvas.

Colette in her beauty shop,
Rue de Miromesnil, Paris, 1932.

While in New York en route back to Paris, Chanel studied the way that the American fashion industry operated and the democratic nature of the department stores, and she established a network of friendly connections with the editors of the fashion magazines.

The writer Colette became the successor to the chair held by her friend Anna de Noailles at the Royal Academy of Belgium. She had long been acquainted with Sert and Misia, and often saw Chanel in Paris and on the Côte d'Azur, where both women had houses—Chanel at Roquebrune, Colette at Saint-Tropez. In addition to her career as a novelist, Colette had long worked as a journalist, and she often wrote articles on fashion in a clear and freeflowing style. In 1932, the year in which Colette opened a boutique selling perfumes and beauty products near the Place Beauvau, one of the many unusual changes in her life that she wittily justified, she also drew a vivid portrait of Chanel in her book, *Prisons et Paradis* (Prisons and Paradises). Colette admired Chanel's determination and drive to achieve perfection in her profession. "With her obstinate energy, the way she takes on a challenge or listens, the defensive attitude that often masks her expression—in all these ways, Chanel is a black bull. Her curly dark head of hair, an attribute of the bull-calf, falls over her forehead to her eyebrows and dances with every motion of her head. It's in the secret domain of her work that we should examine this figure of a thoughtful conqueror."

Vuillard's beautiful charcoal drawing of Anna de Noailles is a preparatory study for his two painted portraits of the illustrious poet, who knew all the writers of her day and received visitors in her bedroom. Vuillard also painted a portrait of the couturiere Jeanne Lanvin, and wanted to paint one of Chanel, but apparently Misia dissuaded him.

THE ONLY TWO WOMEN WRITERS I EVER LIKED WERE ANNA DE NOAILLES AND COLETTE. THE COUNTESS WANTED TO DAZZLE ME. SHE TOOK ON THE FACE OF COCTEAU, AND COCTEAU THE WRITING OF ANNA. SHE WOULD NOT EAT AT TABLE FOR FEAR OF BEING CUT OFF WHILE SHE SPOKE; AND WHEN SHE DRANK, IT WAS LIKE A LECTURER; SHE WOULD MAKE A SIGN OF THE HAND TO INDICATE THAT SHE HAD NOT FINISHED. SHE LOOKED IN MY EYES FOR WHAT PLEASED ME IN WHAT SHE SAID. BESIDES, I WAS THE ONLY PERSON TO NOTICE THAT WHAT SHE WAS SAYING WAS INTELLIGENT. I LIKE COLETTE, WITH HER APOSTLE'S FEET AND HER ACCENT.

Gabrielle Chanel, in Paul Morand, *The Allure of Chanel*

Among the writers and artists recruited by Chanel, the oddest of them all, never mentioned by her biographers, was probably Ilia Zdanevich, also known as Iliazd. A number of exhibitions since his death have explored the range and the diversity of his work. At a very young age, he was one of the most radical poets of the Futurist movement in his native Russia and a perceptive critic of contemporary art, both popular and academic. In his cycle of works he used a transrational language known as *Zaum*, the explosion of the voice. After a year spent in Turkey, where he studied Byzantine art, just one of his many fields of interest, he arrived in Paris in November 1921 and there cultivated his unusual career as a writer, lecturer, impresario, and researcher, and was obliged to hold down a number of jobs in order to make a living. In 1922, he collaborated with Sonia Delaunay on her colored fabrics, and Robert Delaunay produced two charcoal portraits of him. From 1928 until 1934, he worked for Chanel.

In 1940, he published *Afat*, the first of his twenty books illustrated by painters, which he assembled with unsurpassed artistry. This inaugural collection included seventy-six sonnets based on the classic five-accent Russian iamb, plus an extra sonnet, translated here , which was dedicated to Chanel.

Picasso produced wash inscriptions of two Kufic-style arabesques and four etchings of femme fatale figures, shown either sleeping or in the unusual guise of a sphinx.

Robert Delaunay (1885–1941)
Portrait of Iliazd, 1922. Pencil.

Sonnet by Iliazd, dedicated to Gabrielle Chanel,
as it appeared in the copy of *Afat*
numbered 5 and printed specially for Chanel.

Pablo Picasso (1881–1973)
Engraving for *Afat*, 1938.

Габриель Шанель

Мерцающие Ваши имена

    скрывает часто пелена сырая

    моя мольба в костер обращена

    испепеляется не догорая

На Вашем берегу земля полна

    то певчих птиц то клекота то грая

    но вижу протекают времена

    не заполняя рва не расширяя

Живем союзниками но вразброд

    привязаностью сведены не тесно

    мне обещаете провесть совместно

    один из вечеров который год

И не дотерпится предместий Рима

    слабеющее сердце пилигрима

À Gabrielle Chanel

UN VOILE HUMIDE TIENT DISSIMULÉS
    VOS NOMS MIROITEMENT PEUT-ÊTRE MUSE
    BRASIER OÙ MA PRIÈRE DOIT BRÛLER
    JE BRÛLE JE M'ÉPUISE BRAISE OBTUSE
SUR VOTRE BORD LA TERRE S'EST PEUPLÉE
    D'OISEAUX CHANTANTS DE GAZOUILLIS QUI FUSENT
    JE VOIS LE TEMPS S'AMUSE À S'ÉCOULER
    POUR L'UN ET L'AUTRE PAS LA MEME ÉCLUSE
BIEN SÛR NOTRE ALLIANCE TIENT ET NOS
    LIENS RESTENT MOINS LÂCHES QU'IL NOUS SEMBLE
    MAIS NOUS DEVONS PASSER UN SOIR ENSEMBLE
    DEPUIS DES SIÈCLES LA PROMESSE UN MOT
ET LOIN SI LOIN SONT LES FAUBOURGS DE ROME
    LA VOIE LE PÈLERIN CONSUME L'HOMME

Sonnet by Iliazd from *Afat*
French version by André Markowicz

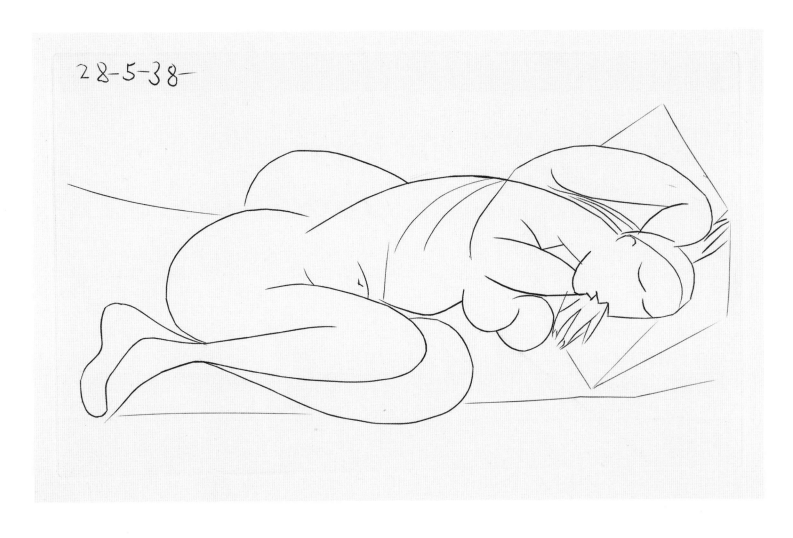

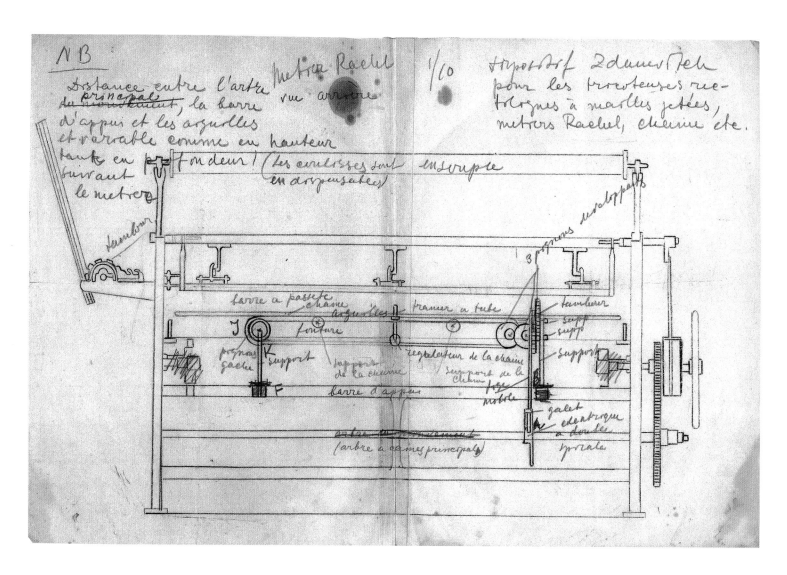

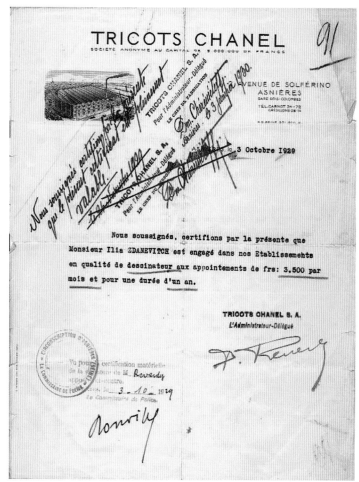

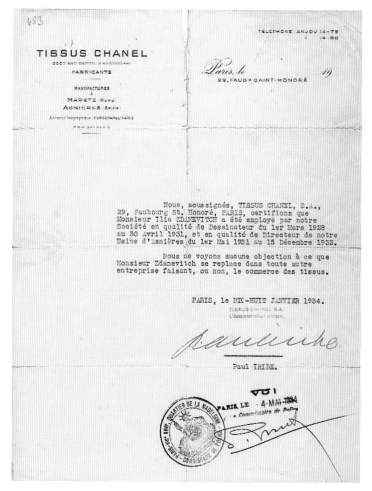

Iliazd left a detailed and fascinating account of his time with Chanel, which describes his endeavors and the life of the company from a personal perspective. Chanel delegated her management powers but maintained aesthetic control over every level of the company. Iliazd was hired first as a draftsman in March 1928; when his contract was renewed in 1929, it was signed by the poet Reverdy, who had reestablished his ties with Chanel. In May 1931, Iliazd was appointed director of the hosiery factory at Asnières, a job that he continued to perform, after an extension of his contract, until January 30, 1934.

This was the period that coincided with the boom in jerseys and knits. The administrator to whom he reported at this time was Paul Iribe, whose technical assistant was François Hugo. Iliazd was in charge of choosing the texture and color of the knits in consultation with Chanel, whom he accompanied many times on her business trips to England. We include here two of the fabric swatches that they retained. He lived in a small home near the plant, where he arrived punctually every day, and he also invented new technology to improve knitting production.

Knitting loom, designed by Iliazd
for Chanel's firm.

Two testimonials for Iliazd issued
by Chanel's firm.

Samples of Chanel fabrics in
woolen jersey and silk jersey.

15

HOMES AND INTERIORS

Drawing room in Chanel's townhouse,
29 Faubourg Saint-Honoré, Paris.
Art et industrie, February 1931.

If costumes are customs, then an outfit must also fit with the place in which one lives. Those who know how to dress and appear outside the home are often equally good at taking care of the insides of their homes. Madame de Pompadour set the tone with the elegance of both her apparel and her residences. "An interior," Chanel noted, "is the natural projection of one's soul, and Balzac was right to place the same emphasis on one's home as one's dress." Upon her arrival in Paris, with tastes formed in her youth by country furniture and a monastic atmosphere, Chanel found some women quite shocking, either because of their clothing (too garish) or their interiors (too cluttered). The first time she paid a visit on Misia, she assumed that her new friend was an antiques dealer, because of the profuse piles of bric-a-brac. Chanel carried out the same process of simplification in interior décor as she did in fashion. The first objects that fascinated her and began to follow her everywhere, as portable as they were decorative, were Coromandel folding lacquer screens. She ultimately owned as many as twenty-one of them, all decorated with white flowers. Misia noticed them as soon as she went to see Chanel, in Quai de Tokyo, the day after they first met. Chanel brought them with her when she moved into the ravishing apartment in the Avenue Gabriel that she shared with Boy Capel.

The villa where she lived for two years after that, on the hill in Garches, surprised her wealthy bourgeois entourage with its beige plasterwork and its shutters painted black. She introduced the use of beige, and later white, in furnishings, well before these colors were embraced by such professional interior decorators as Jean-Michel Frank in Paris and Syrie Maugham in London.

In 1929, she rented the elegant main floor and vast garden of the building at 29 Faubourg Saint-Honoré, a handsome townhouse built at the turn of the eighteenth century by Duchess de Rohan-Montbazon. She hid the historic but excessively ornate green-and-gold boiseries of the long line of high-ceilinged rooms behind a very dignified, but more intimate, enclosure of mirrors and screens, and she arranged to her own taste the period couches and chairs, the crystal chandeliers, the soft carpets, and the velvet curtains, coordinating the décor around three basic colors: white, beige, and a deep brownish black. The guest rooms were used by Picasso, Misia, and Cocteau. In the salon, Stravinsky came to play the piano, as did the musicians of Les Six or the young Igor Markevitch.

The parties and receptions that Chanel held periodically became high points of the season due to their charming setting and illustrious guests. "Twice," wrote the playwright Henri Bernstein in an August 1930 article for *Vogue*, "we dined and danced at the home of our famed and admirable and dearly beloved Gabrielle Chanel, amid the delicate and infinite glittering of the mirrors, the sumptuousness of the lacquerwork, the white profusion of the countless peonies—joyous, subtle, deeply moving celebrations, events that were the envy of thousands (all those who could not be invited despite the vast size of the handsome drawing rooms and halls in the Faubourg Saint-Honoré)—truly magnificent parties, where long ball gowns added emotive grace to the tango."

Chanel claimed to love only palaces or garrets. In 1934, she abandoned her fabulous townhouse for more modest lodgings, and after the death of Iribe, she moved back to the Ritz, her nocturnal refuge. She created a three-room residence above her workspace in the Rue Cambon, an enclave near her office and studio space, served by the same staircase.

It was there that she could be found after her comeback in 1954, in the intimate setting photographed by Robert Doisneau, described by her visitors and now restored and faithfully preserved. A number of carefully selected objects from different centuries and countries—China, Greece, Venice—were displayed openly, creating a superb mélange of nonchalance and imperious refinement. Except for a small canvas by Salvador Dalí depicting an ear of wheat, the earthly symbol of life, there were no paintings.

Even though she was a close companion to many artists, unlike other couturiers such as Doucet, Poiret, and Lanvin, Chanel never collected art, for whatever reason: modesty, determination not to accumulate possessions, or (she said) because her poor eyesight meant that she could not look at paintings without glasses. Between the lacquer screens and the mirrors, the space that was left over was reserved for books, kept within easy reach.

"Above all I bought books; I bought them to read them. Books were always my best friends." She was always given books, by the authors and poets who surrounded her, and she commissioned Maurice Sachs to put together a collection of classics with beige-and-black bindings.

Dining room.
Photograph by Robert Doisneau.

The young architect Robert Streitz was dreaming of building an ideal Mediterranean villa when he met Chanel in Monaco in 1929. She had just completed the purchase of a large parcel of land with a magnificent view of the sun-kissed highlands of Roquebrune. She provided him with the opportunity and the material means to accomplish his dream, while giving him a number of specific directives. In particular, she asked him (and this may have been the first time that she revealed her secret) to visit the abbey of Obazine, examine the magnificent staircase with its worn steps that she used to climb as a weary orphan, and build a replica in her villa.

Twice a month throughout the construction process, she would board the Train Bleu and go to take a look at how work was progressing. She demanded that the roof be covered with old-fashioned round tiles that had to be made by hand; it was necessary to go to neighboring villages to find them. She also wanted the window shutters to be distressed and artificially aged, and the entire house, new though it was, needed to have a patina of age and wear. The entire structure consisted of three wings arranged around a patio paved with sandblasted bricks. The villa was called La Pausa because it stood near a venerable old chapel built on the spot where, according to tradition, Mary Magdalene stopped to rest on her way from Jerusalem.

Beneath its monastic resemblance to Obazine and Royallieu, La Pausa offered all the amenities of a vacation home by the sea, in a bright and fragrant landscape. Even at her age (she was then in her mid-forties), Chanel still loved to climb trees like a country girl, and when she found that there were not enough trees on her land, she ordered some twenty century-old olive trees to be brought all the way from Antibes and transplanted. Beneath their gray and silver foliage, a meadow of lavender unfurled its blue and mauve blossoms, and climbing roses hung from the walls.

"It was the most relaxing and comfortable place I have ever spent time," *Vogue* editor Bettina Ballard recalled in her autobiography. She also described the comforts offered to guests: private bedrooms, grouped in pairs, that could be entered through the boudoir or the bathroom; little cars with drivers who would take guests into town or to the beach to go swimming; a buffet with Italian and French dishes from which guests could help themselves. La Pausa was sold in 1953 to Emery Reves, Churchill's literary agent and a great collector of paintings. His collection was left to the Dallas Museum of Art, with the stipulation that it be housed at the museum in a specially built wing that recreates the original La Pausa in Roquebrune.

La Pausa, Chanel's villa at
Roquebrune on the Riviera, 1938.
Photograph by Roger Schall.

Chanel with François Hugo and Maria Hugo
de Gramont and their son Georges in the
old figtree at La Pausa, Roquebrune, 1938.
Below: Pierre Colle and a lady friend.
Photograph by Roger Schall.

LE FLOT BERCEUR

Les rafles d'or sur le ravin des vagues

Quand les feuillets de la mer se replient page par page

Au bruit du vent

Et des portées des voiles

On commence à s'habituer à tous ces airs

A la couleur de l'eau

Au mouvement des planches

Au goût amer

Le phare a glissé ses ciseaux dans les draps de soleil

Et les bateaux s'en vont sur l'amarre

Le cabestan défait tourne et enroule le port

que ronge un peu la nuit

On chante

Le sable est balayé

Les lumières du fond de la colline ou bien du casino

La voix de l'âne

Pierre Reverdy (1889–1960)
Poem from *Cravates de Chanvre*,
illustrated by Picasso, 1922.
Unique copy with additional watercolors.

Juan Gris (1887–1927)
Portrait of Pierre Reverdy, 1918.

In between her romantic adventures with glamorous foreign partners, Chanel turned her ardor toward a French poet of humble birth, who remained poor and obscure despite his genius and the high regard of his peers. The *tendres liens* (tender bonds) and the *sentiments profonds* (deep sentiments)—to use his own words—that bound Gabrielle to Pierre Reverdy were, along with Obazine, among the secret driving forces of her life.

They met through Misia, and the first and most intense phase of their relationship took place from 1921 to 1924, between Chanel's time with Dmitri and her days with the Duke of Westminster. What divided them were also the things that bound them most fiercely together: their nostalgia for their country childhoods and the scars they caused, their love of the bitter truth, their respect for professionalism and craftsmanship, their passion for and rejection of reality. To Reverdy, a southerner driven by dark passions and Cathar sentiments, "a poet is an oven that burns what is real." It was to him that Chanel owed him her understanding of the Cubist sensibility, which served as an inspiration for her style and which he embodied to the same degree, in his own field, as her friends who were painters and sculptors. His collection, *Cravates de chanvre* (Hemp Neckties), illustrated with three etchings by Picasso, was published in 1922.

Chanel possessed a beautiful edition that the Spanish artist had decorated, page by page, with magnificent watercolors. Reverdy went through a spiritual crisis and, in 1926, withdrew to Solesmes, near the great abbey there. Religious asceticism could not appease his need for the absolute. "Faith," he said, "is a way station on the path to the truth."

From 1929 until 1931, he had passionate encounters with Chanel in Paris and Roquebrune, letting himself to be seduced and bewitched. He fled her influence and her financial assistance and returned to the shadowy solitude that he needed so much, but he never stopped paying impatient calls on her whenever he was in Paris. A few of his later letters still survive. They attest to the fervor and fidelity of his attachment, after the transition "from a great love to an undying friendship."

Chanel outlived him by eleven years, surrounded by his books and manuscripts, which she reread constantly. She made him the sole object of her adoration, as a man and as an artist, and felt outrage at the unjust way he had been forgotten, his genius falling into obscurity, denied the renown that was usurped by others.

Très chère Coco,

Je m'en voudrais de tarder ne fût-ce
qu'une seconde à répondre à votre
petit mot - que je finis de lire. Rien
ne pouvait me procurer un plus
sensible émoi. Vous savez bien que
quoi qu'il advienne et Dieu sait
s'il en est déjà advenu vous ne
pouvez faire que vous ne me voyez
toujours infiniment chère - Aimer
quelqu'un c'est le connaître d'une ...

Among Chanel's sculptor friends, the two leading Cubists were Henri Laurens, whose work was similar to that of Braque, and Jacques Lipchitz, who was closer to Gris. They worked closely at the beginning of their careers, and they shared friendships with the poets Max Jacob and Reverdy. In 1920, Lipchitz produced portrait sculptures of Cocteau, Radiguet, and Gertrude Stein in a classical, non-Cubist style.

The following year, Chanel commissioned him to create one of her, and he employed the same style, with powerful volumes and contrasting shadows and light, aiming for realism. "The portrait itself is not one of my favorites," he said, "but I believe that it captured the appearance of its subject, her strange beauty, and something of her strong personality." He also designed, at Chanel's request, two pairs of andirons, one in human form, the other in animal form, and many plaster models for garden sculptures that were never executed. These decorative works marked a shift in his creative development, introducing curved forms and organic vertical structures that followed his angular and geometric phase.

Pierre Reverdy (1889–1960), French poet.
Photograph by Albert Harlingue / Roger-Viollet.

Jacques Lipchitz (1891–1973)
Portrait of Gabrielle Chanel, 1922.
Bronze.
Photograph by Ali Elai.

Adolphe Mouron Cassandre was renowned in particular for his brilliant work in the realm of posters and typography—he designed the logo of Yves Saint-Laurent—and for his work as a theater designer. But painting was his stubborn obsession, under the strong influence of his friend Balthus. "She [the art of painting] is stingy and gives me little or nothing," he acknowledged. His portrait of Chanel, an old acquaintance, was painted in 1942, and was exhibited in December of that same year at the Galerie Drouin. It was as a guest of Chanel that he was introduced to Reverdy, with whom he became close friends and corresponded at length, and whose portrait he painted in 1943. Thus, the intransigent poet continued to see Chanel even during the most troubled period of his life.

Aside from his collections of poems, Reverdy also left a number of novels, short stories, critical essays, and personal journals that took the form of notes and aphorisms in the style of Friedrich Nietzsche and Nicolas Chamfort. He was a guide to Chanel's conscience as well as her literary adviser, assisting in the editing of her own "Maxims and Aphorisms," a project on which she worked hard, even venturing to publish the results. He wrote to her in 1946: "I congratulate you on the three *pensées* that you sent me; they are quite lovely; the last of the three is perfect, and far above the level one might expect in this genre."

Cassandre (1901–1968)
Portrait of Gabrielle Chanel, 1942.
BALENCIAGA company archives
Oil on canvas.

Cassandre (1901–1968)
Portrait of Pierre Reverdy, 1943.
Oil on canvas.

Overleaf:
"Maxims and Aphorisms" by Gabrielle Chanel,
graphic design by Jean Picart Le Doux.
Vogue, Paris, September 1938.

MAXIMES

Les femmes peuvent tout donner avec un sourire et, avec une larme, tout retirer.

La mode est toujours un reflet de l'époque, mais on l'oublie si elle est bête.

Se déguiser est charmant; se faire déguiser, c'est triste.

Feindre la naïveté vous donne l'air plus sot que l'aveu de votre ignorance.

La coquetterie, c'est une conquête de l'esprit sur les sens.

Les trouvailles sont faites pour être perdues.

La bonté, c'est l'amour: la générosité, une forme de la passion.

La nature vous donne votre visage de vingt ans; la vie modèle votre visage de trente; mais celui de cinquante ans, c'est à vous de le mériter.

La vraie générosité, c'est d'accepter l'ingratitude.

Si vous êtes née sans ailes, ne faites rien pour les empêcher de pousser.

La parure, quelle science! La beauté, quelle arme! La modestie, quelle élégance!

La richesse économe, le faste prétentieux, les libéralités sordides, ce sont les armes les plus sûres du suicide de la fortune.

On peut vous aimer malgré de grands défauts, mais vous haïr pour vraies qualités ou de grandes vertus.

On ne peut ouvrir de barrières que celles que l'on a soi-même fermées.

L'innovation ratée, c'est pénible; la reconstitution, c est sinistre

Pour une femme, trahir n'a qu'un sens : précisément celui des sens.

SENTENCES

Il n'y a que la vérité qui n'ait pas de bornes.

Le dégoût, c'est souvent l'arrière-garde du plaisir, et souvent l'avant-garde.

Le "bon goût" ruine certaines valeurs réelles de l'esprit : le goût tout simple, par exemple.

Il est un moment où l'on ne peut plus toucher à une œuvre : c'est lorsqu'elle en est au pire.

On peut en être réduit à tromper par un excès de délicatesse dans l'amour.

La mode est une reine et parfois une esclave.

Le visage est un miroir où se reflètent les mouvements de la vie intérieure : accordez-lui beaucoup de soins.

Puisqu'il est convenu que les yeux sont le miroir de l'âme, pourquoi ne pas admettre que la bouche soit aussi l'interprète du cœur?

Les seuls beaux yeux sont ceux qui nous regardent tendrement.

La délicatesse de l'oreille n'est pas toujours en rapport avec celle du cœur.

Par la coquetterie, même le cours du temps s'arrête pour les femmes.

Il y a des gestes d'amour et de tendresse qui n'ont de source que dans le dévouement.

Nos maisons sont nos prisons; sachons y retrouver la liberté dans la façon de les parer.

On peut s'accoutumer à la laideur, à la négligence jamais.

C'est le propre d'un esprit faible que de se vanter d'avantages que le hasard peut seul nous donner.

GABRIELLE CHANEL

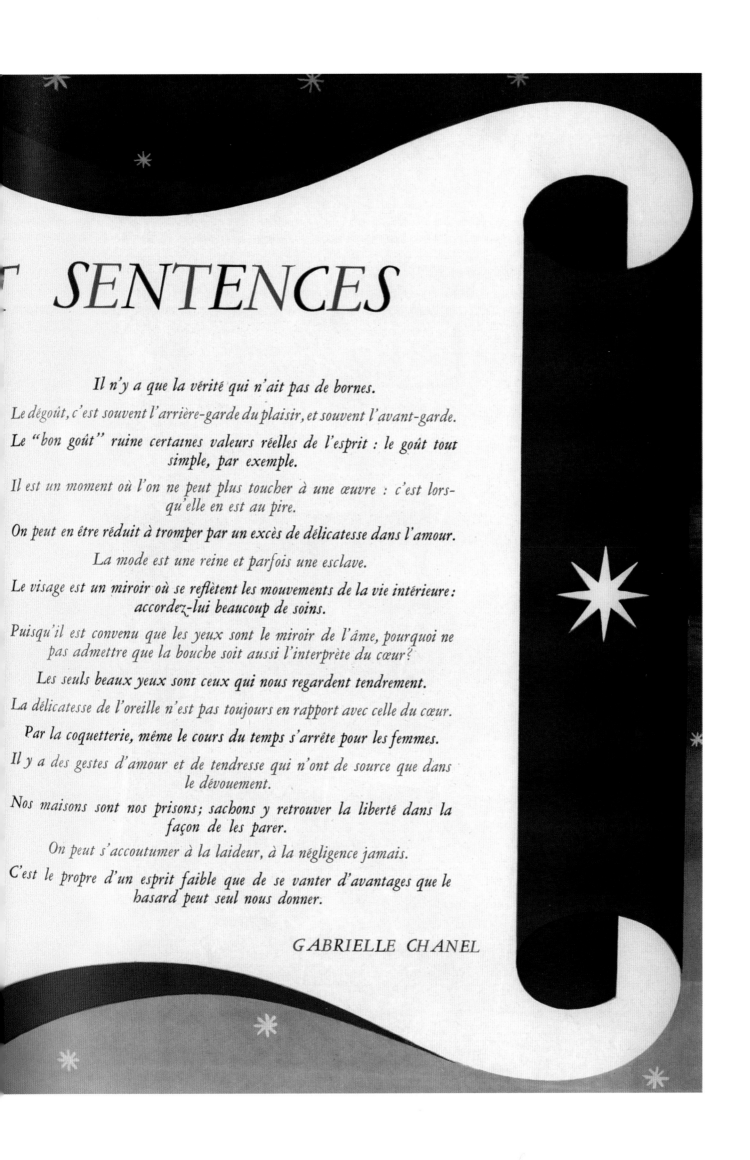

16

VENICE

Gentile Bellini (c. 1429–1507)
Procession of the True Cross in Saint Mark's Square, detail, 1496.
Oil on canvas.

A bout her travels, Chanel spoke little or gave varying accounts. There were only two cities aside from Paris that she considered genuine capitals, true centers of elegance and style: London and Venice. She discovered Venice in the company of Sert and Misia, connoisseurs who showed her the secrets of their beloved city and its dreamlike palaces, to which they easily gained access. Misia took her to elegant boutiques and antique shops, while Sert showed her churches, cathedrals, and museums, focusing in particular on Tintoretto, who echoed his taste for the monumental and the Baroque. "He could lecture for hours," she recalled, "on the use of madder lake in Tintoretto." Venice was a place where water, sky, and stone came together in an unrivaled and musical harmony, and where Chanel underwent a metamorphosis, an initiation into aesthetic joy in the fullness and yearning of the moment.

She abandoned Deauville and Biarritz, resorts that were uncomfortably tied to her memories of Boy Capel, and returned regularly to her beloved lagoon. There she could find refined aristocrats and skilled artisans capable of turning her practical visions into reality. "One day, at the Lido, because I was tired of walking barefoot on the hot sand and because the leather sandals I was wearing were burning the soles of my feet, I asked a bootmaker at the Zattere to trim a piece of cork into a sole and I fastened a pair of straps to it. Ten years later, the window displays of Abercrombie and Fitch in New York were full of cork-soled shoes."

Venice, the city of enchantment, was also a city of funeral rites. In August 1929, three women dressed in white—Misia, Chanel, and Catherine d'Erlanger, flanked by Serge Lifar and Boris Kochno—escorted the last remains of Diaghilev on a black gondola toward San Michele, nicknamed "the island of the dead" because of its cemetery. Nowadays the Lido, the ancient desert coast where Lord Byron rode alone on horseback, is overrun by luxurious beach cabins, and its name is used around the world as shorthand for a fashionable beachfront resort.

In 1931, a relaxed and smiling Chanel posed at the Lido, alongside the handsome couturier Lucien Lelong. She wore a pair of white trousers and a white canvas jacket, a beach outfit that she had designed herself. She considered the shorts that her Italian girlfriends were happy to wear either indecent or comical, and she found the multicolored beach pajamas that were popular that same year throughout the Côte d'Azur to be merely vulgar.

Gabrielle Chanel in Venice.
Vogue, Paris, October 1936.

In 1933, she held a cosmopolitan ball at the charming Hôtel des Bains—once a favorite spot of Diaghilev—for the high-society people who comprised her clientele and who traditionally came to the Lido every year. The lion, both the symbol of Venice and Chanel's star sign, later became an emblem she used to adorn the buttons of her clothing and her jewelry. En route to Venice, she stopped in Milan, and was greeted at the train station by numerous members of the extraordinary Visconti family, who had unanimously fallen in love with her. In October 1936, a journalist for *Vogue* wrote: "It has been years since Venice has experienced such a sparkling season. Dinner parties in the lovely old *palazzi*, the pleasures of sea and sand, the delights of yachting, and every imaginative touch in clothing you could dream of."

Once again, Chanel stood out from the crowd with the boldness and simplicity of her outfit, which seems almost contemporary: a sailor's pullover and cap, a piece of sailcloth knotted around her waist, and, though she was now well over fifty, the perpetual air of a street urchin.

Misia took her first trip to Venice in the fall of 1897, three years before Proust's first visit. At the time, she wrote to Vallotton: "Venice is even more beautiful than I could ever have believed possible, let alone what I might have imagined. . . . There were times when I closed my eyes because I could no longer tolerate such magnificence; at the slightest excuse I would burst into tears of happiness." After so many ecstatic visits, she went back to Venice one last time, in the summer of 1947, for a final pilgrimage. There she met Horst P. Horst and, even though she was sick and nearly blind, she led him through the narrow lanes of the magical labyrinth whose secrets she knew so deeply. Horst photographed her at the Gallery of the Accademia, standing in front of a huge painting by Paolo Veronese, slender and erect in a Chanel suit and flat straw hat, the stunning ghost of a bygone era.

Misia Sert in Venice
wearing a Chanel suit,
summer 1947.
Photograph by Horst.

Misia Sert in Venice.
Photograph by Horst, 1947.

17

JEWELRY

The Empress Theodora,
detail of the mosaic in the choir.
San Vitale, Ravenna, before 547 CE.

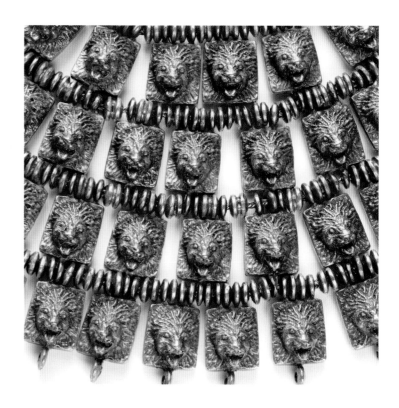

J ewelry is a form of decoration that can rise to the level of great art. All over the world, it is valued as an adornment, an emblem, a treasure, and a sign of prestige. Our fascination with jewels is linked to their ancient magical powers, the mysterious properties of their constituent elements, from rare metals to precious stones. The ancient Egyptians believed that the flesh of the gods was made of gold, and the Book of Revelations describes the walls of the new Jerusalem as being covered with gems.

"Few women," Chanel once said, "know how *not* to wear jewelry." She herself was generally adorned with a profusion of jewelry and thought that it, like perfume, was a necessary part of the art of seduction. She had received exquisite pieces from the Duke of Westminster and from princes of India, but she never wore them except in the privacy of her home, because she preferred to be seen in public wearing ornaments she had designed herself. There were two pieces of jewelry that she never went without, however: the topaz ring that an old woman had given her as a good-luck talisman when she was sixteen, and the beautiful pearl necklace that Boy Capel had given her as a token of his love. Between ostentatious, luxury jewelry and cheap, vulgar trinkets, Chanel wanted to design couture or costume jewelry for a broader clientele, and thanks to her innovation, this became a flourishing field of fashion. Paris at the turn of the century was still the world capital of fine jewelry and embraced the newer trends. The 1925 Exposition Internationale marked a new trend toward color and the return of fine gems, while the 1929 fair at the Palais Galliera saw the rise of diamonds and white metals.

Chanel opened her jewelry atelier in 1924, entrusting it to Count Étienne de Beaumont. She began manufacturing jewelry with Bohemian crystal and paste gemstones, sometimes mixed with real stones.

In 1932, as if to defy the economic crisis, she organized a spectacular presentation of authentic diamond jewelry in collaboration with Iribe. Then she returned to designing artificial pieces with the assistance of such talented collaborators as François Hugo and Fulco di Verdura. Advances in cutting and setting of stones allowed her technicians, under the supervision of Madame Gripoix, to execute nearly all her designs. She drew on a variety of sources and inspirations—oriental, exotic, Egyptian; the discovery of the intact tomb of Tutankhamen with his incredible jewelry had taken place in 1922.

Her tastes ranged from the jewelry of Medici Florence, dating from a period when many artists were trained as goldsmiths, to the sumptuous jewelry of Byzantium. She visited the famous treasury in Munich, the largest collection of jewelry in Europe, and the glittering mosaics of Ravenna, where Empress Theodora stood in glory with her golden crown, dripping with pearls. "Why," Chanel wondered, "does everything that I create become Byzantine?" There are texts that tell us that the wealthy citizens of Constantinople sometimes went out wearing imitation jewelry in gilded bronze, leaving their real gold, pearl, diamond, and enamel jewelry at home.

Detail of a vermeil necklace, made by Robert Goossens under the direction of Chanel, 1960s.

Large vermeil necklace made of 121 lion heads (Chanel's astrological sign), with a carved rock crystal cross at the center, made by Robert Goossens under the direction of Chanel, 1960s.

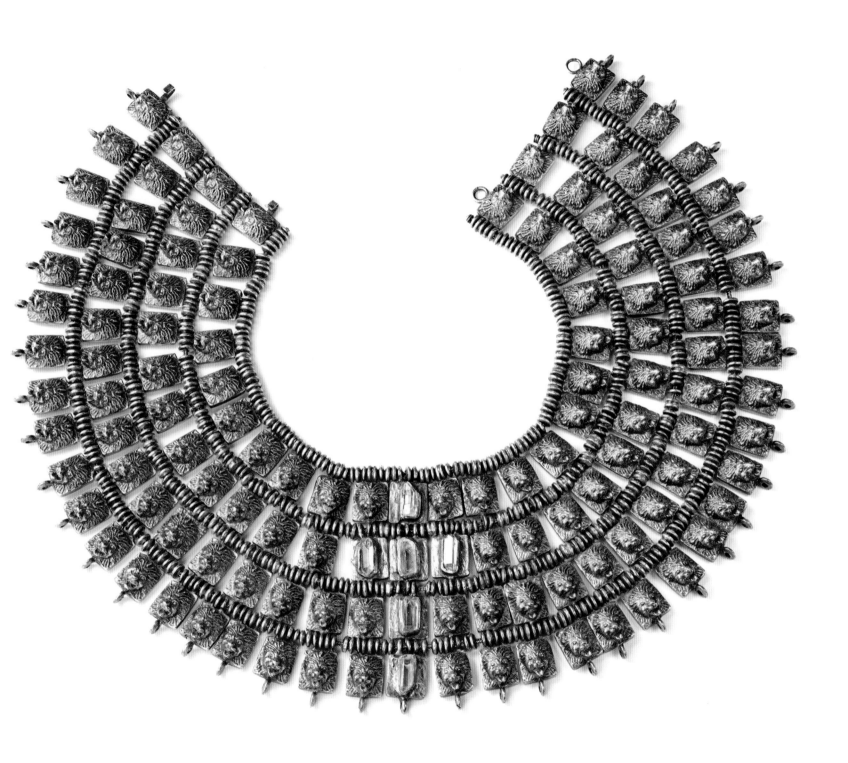

Gabrielle Chanel and Fulco di Verdura, 1937.
Photograph by Lipnitzki.

Pablo Picasso (1881–1973)
Portrait of Comte Étienne de Beaumont, 1925.

Black and white Bakelite cuff bracelets adorned with molten
glass and rhinestones in a cruciform pattern, made by
Robert Goossens under the direction of Chanel, 1960s.

Count Étienne de Beaumont once refused to invite Chanel to his prestigious soirées due to his notions of social exclusivity, but once she became, in her turn, one of the most sought-after hostesses in Paris, he went to work for her, designing long strings of artificial stones with multicolor irregular shapes. Picasso drew several portraits of Beaumont, at the time when the Count was financing the production of the ballet *Mercure*.

Before setting up his own business as a goldsmith in New York, the Sicilian Duke Fulco di Verdura worked for Chanel from 1933 to 1937, first designing fabrics and later as a creator of jewelry. He revived one of the traditional crafts of his country and specialized in enamel bracelets. François Hugo, brother of Jean, technical director of the hosiery factory at Asnières, who appears next to Chanel in a photograph of the fig tree at Roquebrune, also designed jewelry for her. Chanel said, "I get bored with the jewelry made by jewelers; I have François Hugo design my jewelry, based on my own ideas—clips, brooches, all the costume jewelry that you see nowadays in the *galeries* of the Palais-Royal and the Rivoli arcades."

Christian "Bébé" Bérard, who on occasion designed jewelry for Chanel (but much more often for her rival Elsa Schiaparelli), sketched her as she arranged some of her finery on one of her store mannequins.

These wax busts, with sanded skin and perfect makeup, each with a different expression, were set on black marble pedestals and served to display the real diamond jewelry magnificently presented in November 1932 in the private salons of the Faubourg Saint-Honoré. The photographer André Kertész captured the fairy-tale atmosphere of the occasion. The furniture had all been removed, but the glasswork, mirrors, wood paneling, and crystal chandeliers were still in place. In the fireplace—upon whose mantel stood the Greek statue, timeless symbol of beauty—stood the stylized modern andirons by Lipchitz.

Chanel chose gleaming diamonds to express her own dazzling vision of stars, constellations, comets, and the street lights of the Champs-Elysées. Necklaces glittered over bodices made out of moiré ribbons, while tiaras, fringes, ribbons, and brooches shaped like stars or crescent moons shimmered in the hair. The elegant visitors saw the reflections of their faces in the clear glass cases with indirect lighting that protected the fantastic displays.

The gemstones were mounted in invisible settings and the designs were divided into three motifs: bows, stars, and feathers. Many could be taken to pieces and transformed; for example, a necklace could be turned into three bracelets and a hatpin.

Christian Bérard (1902–1949)
Gabrielle Chanel preparing her
exhibition "Bijoux de Diamants", 1932.
Pen and ink.

Princess J.-L. de Faucigny-Lucinge,
Madame Ralli, and Baron de Gunzburg
visiting Chanel's Fine Jewelry exhibition.
Photograph by André Kertész.
Vogue, Paris, January 1933.

The delicate and vibrant pictures in the lavish album accompanying the 1932 exhibition, organized as a charity benefit, were taken by the painter and filmmaker Robert Bresson, a close friend of Gabrielle Chanel.

BIJOUX
DE
DIAMANTS

CRÉÉS PAR

CHANEL

"Noeud" necklace and "Franges" bracelet, created by Chanel for her exhibition *Bijoux de Diamants* (Diamond Jewelry), 1932.

Cover of the press kit for the first jewelry collection.

Text written by Chanel for the press kit.

IN MY PROFESSION, THE MOST DIVERSE MEANS ARE LEGITIMATE AS LONG AS THEY ARE USED ONLY IN THE TRUE SENSE OF FASHION. WHAT MADE ME THINK OF USING IMITATION GEMSTONES IN THE FIRST PLACE, WAS THAT I FOUND THEM TO BE FREE OF ARROGANCE AT A TIME WHEN LUXURY WAS TOO EASY. THIS CONSIDERATION NO LONGER HOLDS IN A PERIOD OF ECONOMIC CRISIS, WHEN AN INSTINCTIVE DESIRE FOR AUTHENTICITY IN ALL THINGS RETURNS, AND THESE AMUSING TRIFLES ARE SEEN FOR WHAT THEY REALLY ARE.

IF I CHOSE DIAMONDS, IT WAS BECAUSE, WITH THEIR DENSITY, THEY REPRESENT THE GREATEST VALUE IN THE SMALLEST VOLUME. I USED MY LOVE OF SPARKLING THINGS TO TRY TO RECONCILE ELEGANCE AND FASHION THROUGH JEWELRY.

Gabrielle Chanel

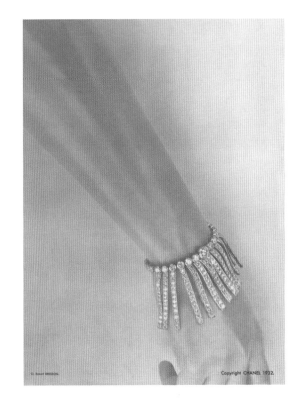

When jewelry is displayed in a glass case it can certainly make up a sumptuous Baroque still life, but it never truly glitters until you see it being worn by someone.

On several occasions Peter Paul Rubens painted his young second wife, Hélène Fourment, in a wedding gown, adorned with all her jewelry. The Flemish artist, influenced by the Venetian style, expressed the luminous intensity of each material, the shimmering of gold on gauze and satin, the translucence of pearls on vibrant flesh. A blossoming sprig in the hair adds natural freshness to the ornate outfit.

Chanel's jewelry showcase,
31 Rue Cambon, Paris, 1938.
Photograph by Roger Schall.

Peter Paul Rubens (1577–1640)
Portrait of Helena Fourment, c. 1630.
Oil on panel.

Chanel's jewelry showcase,
31 Rue Cambon, Paris, 1938.
Photograph by Roger Schall.

Chanel necklace made of glass.
Vogue France, April 1938.

Gold necklace with red, blue, and green
camellias made of glass. Made by Gripoix
under the direction of Chanel, 1938.

The glass and mirrors for which Chanel always had a passion reflect and magnify the dreamlike image of a mannequin adorned with floral jewelry. Leaves and flowers are commonly used motifs in jewelry, for their physical beauty and for their symbolic value. Sometimes naturalistic and sometimes stylized, they were at the height of fashion during the eighteenth century, during the Romantic and Victorian eras, and at the dawn of the modernist style, during the thirties.

Special botanical gardens were created to supply subject matter for the goldsmiths. Combinations of metal, enamel, and colored stones were used to render the curving plant forms and dazzling flowers. Earrings in the shapes of flowers captured the flash and glitter of sunlight.

When Chanel was young, she tried her luck as a singer in the café-concerts of Vichy. Here she is, in this astonishing image, singing songs from the *bal musette* with impertinent glee, while she plays a kidskin and mother-of-pearl Neapolitan accordion. Over her beige jersey pullover with a gold mesh neckline, she dares to wear her most magnificent necklace, with large square-cut emeralds surrounded by round-cut diamonds. Her gold lion's-head jewelry and her imitation Russian and Byzantine crosses with red and green cabochons rival the gems of antiquity in their brilliance.

Historians of jewelry have at times compared the wearing of jewelry to a musical composition, with the metals and gemstones as the instruments, and the wearer and the light as the performers who bring the piece to life.

Choker necklace with large pendant in gold with red and green glass beads and white pearls, made by Robert Goossens under the direction of Chanel, early 1970s.

Cross in gilded bronze, engraved on both sides with a religious figure, inspired by Byzantine reliquary crosses, made by Robert Goossens under the direction of Chanel, 1960s.

Cross in gilded brass adorned with seven red and green glass tiles, suspended from a heavy bail, made by Robert Goossens under the direction of Chanel, 1965.

Chanel playing the accordion. Photograph by François Kollar. *Harper's Bazaar*, September 15, 1937.

18

SOPHISTICATION AND SPECTACLE

Gabrielle Chanel, 1937.
Photograph by Lipnitzki.

Seventy-two *maisons de Haute Couture* took part in the 1925 Exposition Internationale, and this number grew over the following decade. Despite the worldwide economic downturn, ongoing social conflicts, the rise of the Nazis, and international tension, fashion went its sparkling way, as if the fashionable world wished to forget or ignore the impending dangers. Chanel, whose style had seemed to be based on plain short dresses and the gamine look, quite easily adapted to longer dresses and variations on these. In 1933, when Coco Chanel turned fifty, she was at the height of her glory and charm, as can be seen in the numerous portraits taken by the finest photographers of the time. She became known for her simple afternoon dresses, her practical tailored suits in tweed and jersey, for which she had founded the hosiery factory that Iliazd supervised, and her sports and beach outfits, a field in which she had led the way and found spectacular success due to the growing availability of leisure time. But it was evening gowns that best showed off her perfectly honed skills and her capacity for rediscovering purity of form. The two magazines that Iribe published with her financial support allowed her to publicize her ideas on fashion and elegance. "Be a caterpillar by day and a butterfly by night," she advised. "There's nothing more comfortable than a caterpillar and there's nothing better suited for love than a butterfly. You need dresses that creep and dresses that flutter and fly."

At the time, evening gowns vacillated between the neoclassical draped look and the romantic soft look. The return of the traditional waltz after the boldness of jazz coincided with a wave of nostalgia for the Belle Époque and the revival of nineteenth-century bustiers and bustles.

Chanel was highly skilled in her use of transparent fabrics such as tulle, lace, and chiffon, letting gauzy skirts fall from fitted bodices, while staying true to her own quite austere color range: white, black, pink, and navy blue. Ethereal hairstyles, veils and scarves, velvet toques, and floral corsages accompanied these diaphanous gowns. In 1935, Elsa Schiaparelli, her Italian rival, set up shop in the Place Vendôme and infused fashion with surrealist fantasies, radically new materials, unexpected accessories, and acid colors—all treated with her characteristic brio. She began drawing into her orbit artists who had ties to Chanel—Cocteau, Dalí, and Bérard—and put together spectacular collections based on different themes for each season: the seaside, the circus, Commedia dell'Arte, mythology, and music. Chanel reacted. She appeared at parties and costume balls, which were more plentiful and more stunning at the eve of World War II than ever before, she agreed to resume designing costumes for theater, ballet, and cinema, and she also launched such fashion experiments as the gypsy dresses of 1938, with sequined boleros and flashy jewelry, and the tricolor dresses of 1939.

Princess Kathleen Comerford McLoughlin Scherbatow wore with great élan this classically cut suit in black ciré satin. The tailored jacket is fastened at the waist by a button, and at the neck by a large bow. The flat hat is made of the same fabric, and the blouse is made of white ciré satin. The following year, again working with her two signature colors, Chanel matched a sinuous black satin dress with a broad and witty white satin bib with upturned edges.

Chanel tailored suit in black ciré satin.
Photograph by Hoyningen-Huene.
Vogue, Paris, May 1933.

Chanel black satin dress with white satin bib collar.
Photograph by Hoyningen-Huene.
Vogue, New York, September 1, 1934.

198

Hoyningen-Huene shot many portraits of Chanel from 1931 to 1939. The most enchanting of those photographs, because of its classical composition and its modern charm, was the headshot he took in 1939. Framed by her dark hair, for once without a hat, and the white lace collar, her face is a study in sensuous curves. Beneath the imperious arch of her long black eyebrows burn her profound eyes, "a pair of eyes the color of speckled granite," as Colette described them. The flared nostrils and the curving lips quiver with self-restraint. In her June 1936 article on fashion and history, reprinted below with some of her illustrations, Chanel expressed her fascination with "the women who lived between the reigns of Francis the First and Louis XIII"—that is to say, during the period when clothing featured the Spanish-style ruff.

Catherine de' Medici, one of Chanel's heroines, arrived in France with the most beautiful pearl necklace that had ever been seen. De' Medici did a great deal to encourage at the French court the quintessential national art of pastel portraiture. In 1570, her son Charles IX married the charming Princess Elisabeth of Austria, who was sketched and painted by François Clouet. Chanel identified with these compelling figures, "so meticulously dressed that their ruffs and their bodices have as much importance in our eyes as their treaties, their wars, and their family trees. The strange grandeur of fashion becomes a style."

François Clouet (c. 1510–1572)
Elisabeth of Austria, 1571.
Black, red, and white chalk.

Gabrielle Chanel, 1939.
Photograph by Hoyningen-Huene.

PAUL IRIBE WAS THE TRUE CREATOR OF TODAY'S DECORATIVE ART. HE INVENTED ALL OF IT, FOR IT WAS ALL LATENT IN THE PRE-WAR DRAWINGS THAT HE PUBLISHED IN THE FIRST SERIES OF HIS MAGAZINE *LE TÉMOIN*.

André Warnod, *Comœdia*, September 24, 1935

Born to a Basque father and an Andalusian mother, Paul Iribe was exactly the same age as Chanel. At a young age he made his debut as a humorous cartoonist in Parisian illustrated magazines. He quickly displayed his talent and attracted the attention of Dagny Bjørnson, the daughter of the renowned Norwegian author Bjørnstjerne Martinius Bjørnson and the wife of the German publisher Albert Langen. Bjørnson provided Iribe with financing to launch a French satirical magazine similar to the famous Munich publication, *Simplicissimus*, founded by her husband. This was the origin of *Le Témoin*, published from October 1906 to December 1910, which had a major influence on the graphic arts and advertising of its time. Among its contributors were Lyonel Feininger, Juan Gris, Dimitrios Galanis, Pierre-Emile Legrain, Jean Cocteau, Sacha Guitry, and Marcel Duchamp.

In 1908, Iribe published an album of pochoir prints, entitled *Les Robes de Paul Poiret*; this marked Iribe's debut in the world of fashion and led to the popularity of a new style of fashion illustration. "Iribe reigns over the domain of caricature with his wit, and over that of fashion with his grace," Apollinaire observed. In 1911, Iribe married the actress Jeanne Dirys, who drew him into the realm of theater design; Chanel made hats for her. Iribe opened a boutique selling jewelry, fabrics, and furniture, created on commission. He also published books and publicity material. He worked as a war artist during World War I and in 1919 left for the United States, where he married Maybelle Hogan. He became an art director in Hollywood, working with Cecil B. DeMille, but returned to France in 1927, at first taking up residence in Nice, then returning to Paris in 1930.

The exhibition of diamond jewelry in 1932 cemented Iribe's professional and personal relationship with Chanel, who acknowledged his influence and gave him administrative responsibilities. *Le Témoin* resumed publishing from December 1933 to June 1935, with the same caustic verve as before, but now with a reactionary, nationalist, and no longer liberal spirit. The personification of France threatened from within and without bears the features of Chanel.

Iribe also published *La Revue des Sports and du Monde*, which was more open and less partisan; this journal promoted France's luxury industries and artistic professions. Exhausted by his relentless work, Iribe died of a heart attack on September 21, 1935, at Roquebrune. Chanel confided to their common friend, Paul Morand: "I was very fond of Paul Iribe—I felt a genuine tenderness towards him, but now that he is dead, and after so much time has passed, I cannot think without some annoyance of the passionate atmosphere with which he surrounded me. . . . He was a truly perverse being—affectionate, intelligent, calculating, with an extraordinary degree of sophistication."

Paul Iribe (1883–1935):
"Marianne" in the likeness of Gabrielle Chanel.
Cover for *Le Témoin*, 14 October 1934.

le témoin.

DIRECTEUR PAUL IRIBE Nᵒ 32 14 OCTOBRE 1934 LE Nᵒ 1 FRANC 50

LE COMPLIMENT PERDU

WHEN FASHION ILLUSTRATES HISTORY

A strange sense of sympathy and admiration has always drawn me toward the women who lived between the reigns of Francis the First and Louis XIII, perhaps because it strikes me that they were greater than all others, with a magnificent simplicity and a majesty steeped in burdensome duties. But neither [historian Pierre de Bourdeille, seigneur de] Brantôme nor Marguerite de Navarre gave me the moral and physical images that I have formed of them in my head. What I know of them, therefore, I have learned from the portraits of their time; clear, acute, direct portraits—for me, as true as any snapshot.

From Louis XV to the Directoire period, the clothing is full of pleasant compromises and unimaginative revivals. But what force, what character, what a sense of presence and precedence there is in the clothing of the ladies of the sixteenth century. They came into the world aware of their great and demanding duties, duties that required sacrifices, duties that were, morally and socially, so very feminine that it never occurred to them, despite the unmatched strength of their personalities, to question them. To perpetuate, preserve, and exalt their line and everything that made it strong in the present and rich in the future—their men and their offspring—was their destiny and they accepted it with pride in their service.

In order to uphold the prestige of their class, they had to appear as queens presiding over the tournament of life. Their magnificent clothing represented the coat of arms or emblem of their house and their social standing. Armoured with brocade, silk damask, and lace, erect and smiling, real women rather than nude goddesses, they showed the world nothing more than their faces, their white bosoms, and their hands, but it was above all their intelligence and their charm that led the games from a pedestal of wealth. Historians claim with great insistence that within these games they were tremendously free and just as cynical as they were grand, but nowadays who believes historians?

The truth is that they emulated men in nothing; they were exceedingly faithful allies, too faithful to give anything less than their best to the pact of marriage or love, and they were women all the more in that they had the highest interests to defend. I love the fact that Catherine de' Medici was determined to reign as a woman, with a woman's weapons, to the point that she established an entourage, a sort of flying squad of pretty young women, of whom the least we can say is that they were admirably capable, for the purposes of diplomacy, of making use of the same natural weapons that women have wielded in a less considered fashion throughout history, such as fortune and love.

In their spartan attire, they were the pillars of an era, though we cannot say that the artist's hand has stylized the whims of fashion. No, it was these women themselves, proud of their bodies and their poise, who gave a sense of nobility to a style of dress that sculpted them like so many figureheads and placed their small, intelligent heads upon a pedestal of pomp. And so they take their place in the century, a place they occupy with such strength and power that, even now, we cannot stroll through history without brushing against these lively ghosts, so meticulously dressed that their ruffs and their bodices have as much importance in our eyes as their treaties, their wars, and their family trees. The strange grandeur of fashion has become a style. I do not need to know whether it was an architect or a dressmaker who began to impose this line, which belongs to a time when every aspect of the arts was being reborn. Who began it, and were they sculpting the human body or a stone? Who gave the first order? Was it the song of a poet or the practical voice of a woman? Whatever the case, I observe that, even given the inevitable passage of time, a precise and palpable harmony unites all the great artistic creations of that era, which share the trait of an elegance so elevated and a fashion so intense that each and every one of them must take their revenge on humanity by refusing to die.

—Gabrielle Chanel
Article from *La Revue des Sports et du Monde*, June–July 1936

Lucas Cranach the Younger (1515–1586)
Portrait of a Lady, 1564. Oil on panel.

The photographer André Durst, born into a wealthy family from Marseilles, arrived in Paris and soon became a friend of Bérard, Boris Kochno, René Crevel, and Cocteau. He worked for *Vogue* from 1934 to 1940, and created a radically new vision of fashion. He often photographed his models in pairs, posing them in surreal settings with projected shadows, bizarre décor, and distortions of normal perspective. A dress with three flounces in black lace embroidered with white floral motifs is here contrasted with a navy blue tulle dress with floating panels. The double-page image that follows, in which lace and tulle are once again used to flowing and harmonious effect, also features the sumptuous images of André Durst.

Bérard, a painter and theatrical set designer, devoted a great deal of his time and talent to working for couturiers and fashion magazines. Here is one of his illustrations for *Vogue*, where he was a regular contributor from 1935 to 1940, showing two fitted dresses by Chanel, one of them in alternating brown and red panels of satin and sequins, the other in ethereal sky-blue chiffon with a floating scarf, over a dark-blue sheath.

Christian Bérard (1902–1949)
Drawing of two Chanel designs.
Vogue, Paris, October 1, 1937.

Christian Bérard and Gabrielle Chanel at Monte-Carlo.
Photograph by Roger Schall, 1938.

Chanel dresses in navy blue tulle
and black and white lace.
Photograph by André Durst.
Vogue, New York, April 1, 1936.

Chanel white tulle dress with lace bows.
Photograph by André Durst.
Vogue, New York, June 15, 1938.

Chanel dress of white sequin-embroidered lace and net,
and another of black and white lace.
Photograph by André Durst.
Vogue, New York, June 15, 1938.

This is one of Chanel's few relatively extravagant dresses: in black lamé with a golden trellis of squares, with a frothy skirt in bright pink tulle and a sequined bird motif on the bodice.

The photographer Horst posed this model like a living statue in an ornate niche, her arms raised. The long, silvery bodice hugs the slim torso, and the skirt in heavy ribbed crepe flows out over the hips and falls in fluted pleats over the elegantly poised legs.

A twelfth-dynasty Egyptian statuette made of ivory is one of the masterpieces of the Louvre's collection; it transmits an intense sense of life as well as a restrained sense of balance. The elegant tunic with its low-cut bodice is scored vertically by regular groups of four pleats, emphasizing the narrow waist and the curve of the body. There are many notable similarities between Chanel's austere style and the Egyptian artistic canon.

Chanel dress in pink tulle with black and gold lamé.
Photograph by Hoyningen-Huene.
Harper's Bazaar, November 1937.

Chanel dress with ribbed crepe skirt
and silver brocade bodice.
Photograph by Horst.
Vogue, Paris, September 1937.

Christian Bérard (1902–1949)
Gabrielle Chanel in black tulle dresses with ostrich plumes
and sequined bows.
Vogue, Paris, July 1937.

Chanel dresses of tulle.
Bas-relief by Alberto Giacometti.
Setting by Jean-Michel Frank.
Photograph by Man Ray.
Harper's Bazaar, September 1, 1937.

Christian Bérard had a number of friendships and professional relationships with the great couturiers of the time. He felt a skittish
affection for Chanel, who commissioned him to draw her portrait
but never posed for him. The Pavillon de l'Élégance, built and decorated specially for the 1937 Exposition Internationale des Arts et
Techniques dans la Vie Moderne (International Exhibition of Art and
Technology in Modern Life), was the last collective event for Haute
Couture prior to World War II. The pavilion's rooftop restaurant,
the Club des Oiseaux became the setting for the fashion presentations. Bérard sketched Chanel's slim silhouette, as she herself
appeared wearing two of her creations particularly suited to the
surroundings: a gown in black tulle and ostrich plumes with a high,
flowered hat, and a gown in pleated black tulle with silver sequined
bows and a tulle hat with ostrich plumes.

The following year, Bérard used a decorative panel by Boucher as the
backdrop for a Chanel ensemble for spring, a dress made of green
tulle and red flowers with a floating scarf, and a headdress in tulle
and flowers of the same color, with a velvet bow.

Jean Cocteau's *Knights of the Round Table*, Théâtre du l'Œuvre, Paris, October 1937, with Lucien Pascal, Amy Marène, and Samson Fainsilber in costumes by Chanel. Photograph by Lipnitzki.

Jean Cocteau's adaptation of Sophocles' *Oedipus Rex* at the Théâtre Antoine, Paris, July 1937, with Michel Saïanov and Iya Abdy in Chanel costumes. Photograph by Lipnitzki.

In July 1937, Cocteau presented at the Théâtre-Antoine his short play *Œdipe Roi* (based on Sophocles's *Oedipus Rex*), which he had written fifteen years earlier during his classical phase. It marked the debut of the young actor Jean Marais, whom Cocteau had just discovered and whom he would involve from then on in his theater and film productions. For the men's costumes, Chanel designed a crisscrossing network of straps that allowed the contours of their bodies to be seen, and for her friend Iya Abdy, Antonin Artaud's partner in the production of *Cenci*, she created a double necklace made of spools of thread, worn over a spectacular tunic.

In October of that same year, Cocteau staged at the Théâtre de l'Œuvre his new play *Les Chevaliers de la Table Ronde* (The Knights of the Round Table). He personally oversaw the set design and the direction of the play, while faithfully entrusting to Chanel the creation of the varied and sumptuous costumes. Chanel hired Christian Dior as her assistant. Cocteau has described the origin of this esoteric medieval play, which was a departure from his long-standing obsession with ancient Greece: "In 1934, I was quite sick. I woke up one morning, unaccustomed to sleeping, and I witnessed from start to finish this drama in which the intrigue, the period, and the characters were as familiar as they could possibly be. Let me add that I considered them daunting! Three years later, when [Igor] Markevitch affectionately urged me into doing so, I finally managed to bring the play out of the haze in which I had left it suspended, just as things come to us when we are sick, in the morning, forming a continuation of our dreams, stealing from a twilight realm, and inventing an intermediate world to cushion the shock of reality."

Chanel, to the enormous exasperation of Bérard, was a close friend of Dalí. In the fall of 1938, the painter spent four months at her villa in Roquebrune. There he spent time with Pierre Reverdy, "the opposite of me in all things," he said, and since a studio was available, he painted one of his most mysterious canvases, *The Endless Enigma*. In 1939, he conceived for the Ballets Russes of Monte Carlo, under the direction of Massine, a ballet that was revised repeatedly, inspired by the music of Richard Wagner and the story of King Ludwig II of Bavaria, the *Bacchanale*. Chanel designed the costumes with her customary attention to detail. To escape the war, the ballet troupe emigrated in haste to New York, where they performed the show at the Metropolitan Opera, using improvised costumes. In August 1939, while Jean Renoir was in Rome with Luchino Visconti, Dalí took refuge in Arcachon. Chanel joined him in September for a two-week vacation. They had similar points of view on a number of issues, Dalí observed, but their spiritual natures were different. "Chanel's originality was the opposite of mine. I have always shamelessly exhibited my thoughts, while she neither conceals hers nor shows them off, but instead dresses them up. For her, Haute Couture has always had a biological impulse, an origin in modesty; she has the best-dressed body and soul on Earth."

Gabrielle Chanel with Salvador Dalí on the stairs at
31 Rue Cambon, Paris, 1938.
Photograph by Roger Schall.

The ballet *Bacchanale*, 1939,
with costumes designed by Dalí and executed by Chanel.
Photograph by Horst.

Visconti, the great Italian director, was a member of the illustrious family that had governed Lombardy for centuries. He had three brothers and three sisters, all of whom were remarkably distinguished, resembling, it has been said, the medallions by Pisanello depicting their ancestors. His mother, Carla, whom the family all adored, proved to be a particularly charming educator and caregiver. Their father, Giuseppe, Duke of Modrone, restored the entire village of Grazzano, his country fiefdom, and designed medieval dresses for his daughters and the local peasants to wear. During his earliest stays in Paris, Luchino Visconti met and was captivated by Chanel, and their brief liaison was transformed into a lasting friendship. He admired her rare blend "of feminine beauty, masculine intelligence, and fantastic energy." In the photographs that depict them together, the dazzling couturiere, leaning on his arm, turns a fond gaze up toward the young and pensive prince, many years her junior. They traveled extensively together, to Paris, Milan, Venice, Rome, and Capri.

In 1936, Visconti determined that his career was to be in film, his great passion since childhood. Chanel, who had superior intuition, introduced him to Jean Renoir, who hired him as an assistant on *Les Bas-fonds* (The Lower Depths) and, in particular, on *Partie de campagne* (Day in the Country). This experience was crucial to Visconti's political, artistic, and moral development. He never stopped thinking of Renoir as his teacher and mentor. "I recall his humane generosity, his kindness toward people and their work. I could always talk to him like a brother." In the spring of 1939, Renoir directed the actress Nora Grégor in *La Règle du jeu* (The Rules of the Game), the film that he wanted to make "classic and poetic," in keeping with his naturalist experiments; he asked Chanel to design the costumes. This magnificent production—which in time became, to use the words of François Truffaut, "the credo of movie lovers, the film of films"—premiered in July of that year, and was roundly jeered because it offered the public a clear-eyed portrayal of the moral issues of the time. A short while later, in August, Renoir accepted an invitation to make a film of Giacomo Puccini's *Tosca* in Italy. He was warmly welcomed in Rome by Visconti, who helped write the screenplay, showed Renoir around the city, and introduced him to his friends. This was the last meeting between the two directors, but their mutual esteem remained firmly established.

Gabrielle Chanel with Luchino Visconti, 1938.

Jean Renoir with Nora Grégor in a Chanel dress, in the Jean Renoir film *The Rules of the Game*, 1939.

19

RETIREMENT

Gabrielle Chanel between coromandel screens in her
apartment at 31 Rue Cambon, Paris, 1937.
Photograph by Lipnitzki.

On September 3, 1939, after the declaration of war, Chanel shut down her *maison de couture*, leaving only her boutique of accessories and perfumes. She believed that there was no more need for dresses and gowns. Her gesture was matched by Reverdy, who stopped writing during the dark years. In Paris, she became a recluse in her apartment on the Rue Cambon, where the dancer and choreographer Serge Lifar was her neighbor. "In that period, I spent long evenings talking with Chanel who, as a result of her inactivity, had returned to her first loves, music and song. . . . She would also read me the French classics."

She carried on a discreet relationship, in Roquebrune and especially in Switzerland, with a German diplomat whom she had met years earlier in society circles, a last and ill-advised love affair that put her under suspicion after the Liberation, despite her powerful connections. It prolonged her exile and only exacerbated her bitterness. In Switzerland, she loved Lausanne and its lakeside villas; she purchased a simple and quite ordinary villa on a hillside, which she later furnished with chairs made by the marvelous craftsman Diego Giacometti, brother of the sculptor Alberto. In 1946, she traveled to New York to review the marketing contracts for her perfumes, a major source of revenue.

In July 1949, she graciously received a visit from the young Italian director Franco Zeffirelli, sent by Luchino Visconti. In his autobiography, Zeffirelli recalled her charm and generosity, yet another testimonial to those qualities. He described dazzling walks with her through Paris, the meetings she arranged with Roger Vadim and Christian Bérard, and the gifts she gave him when he left. In the winter of that same year, she withdrew to the Engadin Valley in the Swiss Alps, with the intention of working on a book about her life—or her legend. Paul Morand wrote down her recollections and her recriminations, while preserving "that torrential voice, pouring out like lava," the bold energy still compressed within that "volcano from the Auvergne that Paris wrongly believed to be extinct."

In 1951, she stayed at the Waldorf Astoria Hotel in New York, with the Baroness Marguerite van Zuylen, her closest confidante during her retirement. Horst took some photographs of her, but they were not published, because, as he observed, without her work, Chanel—her eyebrows plucked, her hair faded and drab, with an absent air—was no longer the same woman he had once photographed. Her friends died one after another: Dmitri in 1942, Sert in 1947, Misia in 1950, the Duke of Westminster in 1953. She sold her villa in Roquebrune and secretly made preparations for a comeback, with the support of Pierre and Paul Wertheimer and the assurance of opportunities in the United States, thanks to the contacts she had renewed.

With her canny commercial flair, she chose the right moment. After the skimping and constraints of wartime, the revolution that swept through fashion in 1947, Christian Dior's New Look—flared skirts and corseted waistlines—struck her as a striking but artificial revival of the Second Empire, which she rejected with all the force that she had once reserved for Poiret's orientalism and which in any case grew more tired and less "new" with every seasonal variation. The year 1949 witnessed the birth of *prêt-à-porter*—ready-to-wear—which was haute couture adapted to provide fashion for a wider public. This required a modern yet classic approach to apparel, which Chanel felt she was capable of providing, given the feminine acuity of her tastes and her mastery of her craft.

Gabrielle Chanel with Valentine Lawford in his 1948 MG, at Oyster Bay on Long Island Sound, 1951. In the background: Baroness Maggie Van Zuylen. Photograph by Horst.

20

RETURN AND RECOGNITION

Marie-Hélène Arnaud in a Chanel
tailored suit in navy blue jersey from
the Haute Couture collection,
Spring–Summer 1954.
Photograph by Henry Clarke.
Vogue, Paris, March 1954.

At the age of seventy, on February 5, 1954, Chanel made her return. Her collection, which her audience expected to find spectacular, appeared outmoded and disappointing. She recognized her mistake, and instead of taking it to heart, she simply felt motivated to work harder. She pulled herself together. Previously unpublished photographs taken at this time by the sculptor and art director Alexander Liberman reveal her determined and self-aware attitude and her strong powers of concentration. Criticized in France and, more disturbingly to her, in Great Britain, she still enjoyed the support of the American press. In March, American *Vogue* published on its opening pages the navy blue jersey suit with reversible cuffs that had opened her runway show. It was worn proudly, with hands in pockets and a beribboned boater, by the young and ravishing Marie-Hélène Arnaud, who was the living image of Chanel. The white linen blouse with a black satin bow was fastened to the skirt with buttons. Bettina Ballard, the fashion editor responsible for the article, purchased the outfit and wore it in New York, where it was seen by the biggest names in fashion.

By 1956, Chanel had reclaimed her empire and her supremacy. "The most surprising thing," journalist Françoise Giroud pointed out, "was her resurrection and the intelligence that she used to bring it about." The woolen tailored Chanel suit enjoyed the same universal success as her little black dress had in an earlier time. She began to create jewelry again, introduced a style of flat-heeled two-toned shoe in beige and black, comfortable to walk in and intended to make the feet look small, and designed her signature quilted bag with a gold-chain shoulder strap. That same year, in the fall of 1957, she returned to the United States in the company of Georges Kessel and was awarded the Neiman Marcus Award for Distinguished Service in the Field of Fashion in Dallas, honoring the most influential fashion designers of the century. Trade publications as well as mass-market magazines reported twice yearly on the ritual of her runway presentations and devoted enthusiastic pages to her unsurpassed artistry and her legendary personality.

"Why," *Elle* asked on November 17, 1958, "do Michèle Morgan and ten million women vote for Chanel nowadays?" She dressed society ladies and actresses, who became her models on the stage and screen, but her style, as she wished, also reached the streets, because it managed to create a synthesis between the timeless and the contemporary, between social distinction and democratic conformity. She imparted her secrets in short and snappy maxims that can be applied well beyond the domain of fashion: "Always remove, never add—never a button without its buttonhole—the back just as perfectly finished as the front."

The death of Reverdy, in 1960, plunged her into a loneliness that was as inevitable as it was dreaded. Her friends were dead—"it was the artists," she said, "who taught me rigor"—and she no longer had anyone but acquaintances, the result of her passion for work and her harsh judgments. In 1965, she condemned the miniskirt, because she did not find the knees aesthetically pleasing, and because she believed that fashion should not surrender to the pressure of youth, but should instead make all women feel young and well-dressed, comfortable in their bodies, confident in their future. She spent her last years at the peak of her profession, thanks to her absolute mastery of cut and material, using flowing chiffons or fitted lamés in a sort of tribute to oriental styles, Tibetan or Chinese, along with a new sense of color, still completely natural in its sophistication: the beige of skin, the red of blood, the green of plants, the blue of the sky, and the gold of the sun. Gabrielle Chanel died on a Sunday, January 10, 1971. The funeral service, held at the church of La Madeleine in Paris, brought together all the couturiers she had influenced. Her grave is in the cemetery of Lausanne, Switzerland. On her tombstone, set among white flowers, a row of lion's heads—representing her star sign of Leo—guards her resting place.

Gabrielle Chanel in her Paris apartment,
31 Rue Cambon, 1954.
Photograph by Alexander Liberman.

Gabrielle Chanel, April 1965.
Photograph by Cecil Beaton.

Chanel shirtdress in red jersey.
Vogue, New York, January 1955.

Joanna McCormick in a Chanel tailored suit in white and gold
silk brocade with navy blue and gold velvet trimmings.
Photograph by Henry Clarke.
Vogue, Paris, April 1957.

Alongside her daytime tailored suits and evening gowns and accessories, Chanel also created light, short dresses to be worn without a hat, for a cocktail party or a garden party. The floral print on this diaphanous silk chiffon dress is echoed by the flowers embroidered in relief on the strapless bodice. This photograph was taken in the greenhouses of the Vilmorin family, at Verrières-le-Buisson, by Henry Clarke, a fashion photographer with a sure sense of elegance, sometime after 1950.

Sandro Botticelli's famous *Birth of Venus* was painted for a Medici country villa. According to the ancient myth revived by Florentine humanism, Venus was the embodiment of Beauty, and the wind gods are pushing her toward the shore beneath a shower of roses. The image of the nymph of spring preparing to wrap her in a crimson cape is a wonderful symbol of costume and its transfigurative function.

Marie-Hélène Arnaud in a Chanel print dress in silk muslin
from the Haute Couture collection, Spring–Summer 1957.
Photograph by Henry Clarke.
Vogue, Paris, May 1957.

Sandro Botticelli (1445–1510)
The Birth of Venus (detail), c. 1482.
Oil on canvas.

Chanel dress in silk organdy.
Photograph by Guy Bourdin.
Vogue, Paris, May 1960.

Chanel sheath dress in black muslin and sequins.
Photograph by Henry Clarke.
Vogue, Paris, March 1961.

Two springtime ensembles by Chanel: on the left, a soft gray and pink silk organdy dress, its bodice highlighted by two moiré ribbons; on the right, a sheath dress with black sequins, like a relic from the Roaring Twenties, but with an accentuated waistline.

They are both finished off by a flowing scarf or veil over the shoulders, and are photographed in two different fashion styles—strict and pure by Henry Clarke, sensual and calculated by Guy Bourdin.

Marie-Hélène Arnaud in a suit from the Chanel Haute
Couture collection, Spring–Summer 1959. Black silk tweed
with a white surah blouse.
Photograph by Henry Clarke
Vogue, Paris, April 1959

Paule de Mérindol in a suit from the Chanel Haute Couture
collection, Spring–Summer 1959, outside the shop at
31 Rue Cambon. Beige tweed trimmed with navy grosgrain.

Romy Schneider in a gold lamé tunic dress by Chanel, in the Luchino Visconti film *Boccaccio '70*, 1962.

Romy Schneider at a fitting with Gabrielle Chanel in the studio at 31 Rue Cambon, 1960. Photograph by Giancarlo Botti.

"Nowadays," the French weekly *Elle* reported in November 1958, "everyone in the movies wants to have their costumes made by Chanel." Many young actresses who were among her clients agreed to pose for fashion magazines, and the directors of the French New Wave wanted to work with her. In 1958 she created the stunning ensembles that Jeanne Moreau wore in Louis Malle's *Les Amants* (The Lovers), and in 1961 she designed the dreamy outfits for Delphine Seyrig in *L'Année dernière à Marienbad* (Last Year at Marienbad), the eclectic film by Alain Resnais with a screenplay by Alain Robbe-Grillet. An unpredictable embodiment of memory or imagination, Seyrig sometimes changed her outfit and her personality in the course of a single scene.

Romy Schneider, the daughter of Austrian actors, debuted at an early age in the *Sissi* series of films. Visconti discovered her in Paris in 1961, recognized her talent, and cast her in a tough role in a theatrical production to develop her personality. The following year, he cast her in a central role in "Il Lavoro" (The Job), one of the three segments of the film *Boccaccio '70*. The plot, based on a short story by Guy de Maupassant, was transposed into the social circles of Milan, which Visconti knew very well. The film, a social satire, is a masterpiece for its complexity, technique (color, closeups, depth of field), and impressive use of its star. Visconti asked Chanel to design costumes for Schneider, but also to work with her, to pass on the secrets of elegance, something Chanel was particularly happy to do because she liked and admired the young actress. Here Schneider is depicted wearing magnificent jewelry, adjusting the details of her seductive image before the mirror.

hanel was a pioneer in introducing beach pajamas, and she was comfortable wearing trousers in the country, as when she climbed trees at Roquebrune, but she absolutely refused to wear them in the city. Chanel trousers, which became increasingly numerous after 1964, were designed only as intimate evening wear. Here is a straight-legged pair from 1969. Worn with a collarless gold-and-chartreuse lamé jacket with glittering braidwork, plus matching sandals, they create a particularly luxurious impression with a deceptively simple structure.

A Far Eastern influence can often be detected in the work of Chanel, but especially at the beginning and the end of her career. Silk in China is as ancient as linen in Egypt, and its exquisite weave gives a dignified air of sophistication, with a symbolic meaning. Dragon or mandarin robes, worn especially by men but also by women, have braidwork around the collar, and their embroidered motifs include water, mountains, clouds, and dragons. The dominant color is blue, but they also exist in red, yellow, orange, turquoise, and brown. The one shown here, now in London, shows magnificent workmanship, with the same sunny and green tones as the Chanel evening suit. The yellow sleeves with the flared cuffs were probably a later addition.

Chanel suit, jacket and pants in
gold and chartreuse lamé brocade.
Photograph by Henry Clarke.
Vogue, Paris, April 1969.

Dragon robe, embroidery on satin weave silk.
Late-eighteenth to middle of the nineteenth century.
China, mid-Qing Dynasty.

21

INFLUENCE AND LEGACY

Dorothy Mc Gowan in a suit from the Chanel
Haute Couture collection, Fall–Winter 1960.
White tweed with navy braided wool trim.
Dorothy + curé, Paris, 1960.
Photograph by William Klein
Vogue, Paris, October 1960

Chanel approached a number of authors to write her memoirs, but no biography was published during her lifetime. "The life that you lived is not particularly significant," she declared, "but the life you dreamed of, that is the important thing, because it continues after your death." Cristóbal Balenciaga, the couturier that she rightly admired more than any other, maintained with her "a rivalry without jealousy." He said, "Chanel is an eternal bomb that none of us can hope to defuse." She remains ever-present through the influence of her legend and the power of her style.

The fashion house that she founded continues to operate from the same premises, under the same name, with her logo and typography unchanged, and with the incredible enclave of her personal apartments intact. The current chairman belongs to the Wertheimer family, which has operated the perfume company since 1924 and all the Chanel subsidiaries since 1954. The runway shows of Chanel fashion collections still bear her name, and they take place beneath the magnetic gaze of her much-enlarged image. Horst photographed her in 1939 examining her famous Watteau-inspired suit, as if her intense eyes were gazing beyond to see all the variations of that design that she and her successors would derive from that painter who was so bewitched by clothing.

Chanel had long wanted to create a perfume that would epitomize her work and speak to her courage, to be named "Coco." It was created, in 1984, by the alchemist of the *maison*, Jacques Polge, whose expertise, acquired at Grasse in the tradition of Ernest Beaux, was combined with great knowledge and sensitivity. It was a complex perfume, with notes of amber and flowers enhanced by a hint of spiced leather. The fruit and floral head note balanced the contrasting tones, and the amber bottom note, with its warm, woody nuances and its touch of leather, was created in the style of the older Chanel perfumes that are no longer commercially available. Coco revisits the oriental scents "which sing of transports of the spirit and the senses" and harmonizes beautifully with the clothes and jewelry still produced under the name of Chanel, that timeless magician.

Gabrielle Chanel with her model Muriel Maxwell wearing a black silk velvet suit with neck ruff adapted from Watteau.
Photograph by Horst.
Vogue, New York, September 15, 1939.

Bottle of Coco perfume.
Photograph by Daniel Jouanneau.

Page 244:
Inès de La Fressange in a white silk
Chanel outfit from the Haute Couture
collection, Spring–Summer 1985.
Photograph by Horst.
Vogue, Paris, March 1985.

Page 245:
Antoine Watteau (1684–1721)
Pierrot, Formerly Known as Gilles, c. 1718–1719.
Oil on canvas.

The modern poetics of fashion was launched by Baudelaire, spread throughout Proust's entire oeuvre and converted into a system by Roland Barthes. In his frequently quoted article from 1968 on the necessary relationship between style and fashion, between lasting *chic* and the ephemeral *neuf* (new), Barthes wrote: "Chanel always works on the same model which she merely 'varies' from year to year, as one might 'vary' a musical theme; her work says (and she herself confirms it) that there is an 'eternal' beauty of woman, whose unique image is relayed to us by art history."

Hence the comparisons, over the course of this book, between her most significant creations as seen by the finest photographers and examples of artwork ranging from ancient Egypt to Cubism and Matisse. Chanel's variations are created through cut, fabrics, and accessories; they are based on timeless structures, which can be endlessly adapted and passed on.

These basic forms have survived for many years, thanks to the excellence of the Chanel ateliers and the loyalty of the house's traditional artistic consultants. Since 1983, these iconic styles have been entrusted to the imagination of a respected designer, Karl Lagerfeld, who has a particular passion for the eighteenth century and who accepted the challenge while continuing to produce work under his own name. His challenging mission consists not of borrowing eclectically, but rather of creating brilliant variations on the classic themes of his illustrious predecessor. The difference, which marks the modern transition from couturiers to stylists, is that he begins with a graphic approach, while Chanel, scissors in hand, always tested her designs on the living body.

Raincoat from the early eighteenth century.
Vogue, New York, October 2007.

Raquel Zimmermann in a pale pink taffeta dress from the
Chanel Haute Couture collection, Fall–Winter 2007.
Photograph by David Sims.
Vogue, New York, October 2007.

INDEX OF ILLUSTRATIONS

ARTS AND ARTISTS

ANCIENT ROME:
The Initiate, Pompeii, Villa of the Mysteries (detail)—p. 12
Primavera, wall painting—p. 116

BELLINI, Gentile—p. 172

BÉRARD, Christian—pp. 185, 204, 211

BOLDONI, Giovanni—p. 33

BONNARD, Pierre—p. 64, 67

BOTTICELLI, Sandro—p. 231

BOUCHER, François—p. 21

BRAQUE, Georges—p. 61

BYZANTIUM:
Mosaic in the choir of Saint Vitale, Ravenna—p. 178

CASSANDRE—pp. 168, 169

CHINA:
dragon robe—p. 239

CLOUET, François—p. 198

CRANACH, Lucas, the Elder—p. 82

CRANACH, Lucas, the Younger—p. 202

DAVID, Jacques-Louis—p. 23

DEGAS, Edgar—pp. 28, 47

DELAUNAY, Robert—p. 152

EGYPT:
Offering bearer—p. 8

GOYA, Francisco—p. 22

GRASSI, Giovannino de'—p. 14

GREECE:
Antigone brought by two guards before Creon—p. 96
Kore from Samos—p. 11

GRECO, El (attributed to)—p. 135

GRIS, Juan—pp. 78, 79, 165

HUGO, Jean—p. 126

HUGO, Valentine—p. 80

INGRES, Jean Auguste Dominique—pp. 24, 25, 27

IRIBE, Paul—p. 201

LAURENCIN, Marie—p. 102

LAURENS, Henri—p. 88

LÉGER, Fernand—p. 118

LIPCHITZ, Jacques—cover illustration, p. 167

MATISSE, Henri—pp. 48, 49, 139

MODIGLIANI, Amedeo—p. 108

MIDDLE AGES:
Saint Modeste—p. 136
Uta of Naumburg—p. 13

PICASSO, Pablo—pp. 56, 71, 72–73, 74, 80, 85, 105, 125, 153, 183

RENOIR, Pierre-Auguste—p. 31

REVERDY, Pierre—p. 164

RUBENS, Peter Paul—p. 188

SARGENT, John Singer—p. 32

SEM—p. 86

TITIAN—p. 16

VAN DYCK, Anthony—p. 17

VELÁZQUEZ, Diego—p. 18

VUILLARD, Édouard—p. 149

WATTEAU, Antoine—p. 20, 245

PAGE BY PAGE

p. 6—Chanel wearing one of her designs, 1937. Photograph by Sir Cecil Beaton. Courtesy of the Cecil Beaton Studio Archive at Sotheby's.

p. 8—Offering bearer, Egypt, Middle Kingdom, Eleventh Dynasty, stuccoed and painted wood. Height 3.5 ft. (1.08 m). Paris, Musée du Louvre. © RMN / Les frères Chuzeville

p. 11—The Kore of Samos, first half of the sixth century BCE, marble, height 6.4 ft. (1.95 m). Paris, Musée du Louvre, Department of Greek, Etruscan and Roman Antiquities. © RMN / Hervé Lewandowski

p. 12—The Initiate, Pompeii, Villa of the Mysteries, c. 70–60 BCE (detail). © Scala, Florence

p. 13—Uta of Naumburg, Naumburg Cathedral, c. 1260. © akg-images / Erich Lessing

p. 14—Giovannino de' Grassi (1350–1398), *Two Women Playing Music*, ink and watercolor on vellum, 10.1 x 7.3 in. (25.7 x 18.7 cm). Bergamo, Biblioteca Civica, Codex VII, 14, folio 5 recto. © Piero Borgognone, Bergamo

p. 16—Titian (c. 1489/1490–1576), *Isabella of Portugal, Wife of Charles V*, c. 1548, oil on canvas, 46 x 38.5 in. (117 x 98 cm). Madrid, National Museum of the Prado. © akg-images / Erich Lessing

p. 17—Anthony Van Dyck (1599–1641), *The Marchesa Doria*, 1625, oil on canvas, 94 x 67 in. (239 x 170 cm). Paris, Musée du Louvre. © RMN / Hervé Lewandowski

p. 18—Diego Velázquez (1599–1660), *The Infanta Maria Theresa*, c. 1653, oil on canvas, 50 x 38.7 in. (127 x 98.5 cm). Vienna, Kunsthistorisches Museum. © Kunsthistorisches Museum, Wien / KHM, Vienna

p. 20—Antoine Watteau (1684–1721), *Standing Woman from Behind, About to Start Dancing*, three pencils, 9.6 x 4.2 in. (24.4 x 10.7 cm). Haarlem, Teylers Museum. © Teylers Museum Haarlem The Netherlands

p. 21—François Boucher (1703–1770), *The Marquise de Pompadour*, 1759, oil on canvas, 34.2 x 25.9 in. (87 x 66 cm). London, The Wallace Collection. © The Wallace Collection, London

p. 22—Francisco Goya (1746–1828), *The Countess of Carpio, Marquesa de la Solana*, c. 1794, oil on canvas, 71.2 x 48 in. (181 x 122 cm). Paris, Musée du Louvre. © RMN / Jean-Gilles Berizzi

p. 23—Jacques-Louis David (1748–1825), *Madame Récamier*, begun in 1800 and left incomplete, oil on canvas, 68.5 x 96 in. (174 x 244 cm). Paris, Musée du Louvre. © RMN / Rights reserved

p. 24—Jean-Auguste-Dominique Ingres (1780–1867), *Madame de Senonnes*, 1814, oil on canvas, 41.7 x 33 in. (106 x 84 cm). Nantes, Musée des Beaux-Arts. © RMN / Gérard Blot

p. 25—Jean-Auguste-Dominique Ingres (1780–1867), *Study for the dress of Baroness James de Rothschild*, black chalk highlighted with white chalk on brown paper, 12.9 x 9.8 in. (33 x 25 cm). Montauban, Musée Ingres. © Musée Ingres, Montauban

p. 27—Jean Auguste Dominique Ingres (1780–1867), *Princess de Broglie*, 1853, oil on canvas, 47.7 x 35.7 in. (121.3 x 90.8 cm). New York, The Metropolitan Museum of Art. © Bridgeman Giraudon

p. 28—Edgar Degas (1834–1917), *Princess Pauline de Metternich*, c. 1861, oil on canvas, 16 x 11 in. (41 x 29 cm). London, The National Gallery. © The National Gallery, London, dist. RMN / National Gallery Photographic Department

p. 31—Pierre-Auguste Renoir (1841–1919), *The Parisienne*, 1874, oil on canvas, 63 x 42 in. (160 x 106 cm). Cardiff, National Museum of Wales. © National Museum of Wales / The Bridgeman Art Library

p. 32—John Singer Sargent (1856–1925), *Madame X (Madame Gautreau)*, 1884, oil on canvas, 82 x 43 in. (210 x 110 cm). New York, The Metropolitan Museum of Art, Arthur Hoppock Hearn Fund, 1916. © Geoffrey Clements / Corbis

p. 33—Giovanni Boldoni (1842–1931), *Madame Charles Max*, 1896, oil on canvas, 80 x 39 in. (205 x 100 cm). Paris, Musée d'Orsay. © RMN

p. 35— Countess Greffuhle, née Élisabeth de Caraman-Chimay, in a Worth ball gown, 1896. Photograph by Paul Nadar. Paris, Caisse nationale des monuments historiques et des sites. © RMN

p. 36—"Mélodie" dress, 1912. UFAC, Paris. © Rights reserved

p. 37—"Battick" coat, 1911. Photograph by Edward Steichen. Published in *Art et décoration*, April 1911. © Selva / Leemage. Permission of Johanna T. Steichen

p. 38—Obazine Abbey (Corrèze). © Clare Fenton

p. 40—The interior staircase of Obazine Abbey. © Jérôme Gautier

p. 41—Pavement of Obazine Abbey. © Abbaye d'Obazine / Clare Fenton

p. 42—Gatehouse of Royallieu Abbey. © Studio Vogue

p. 43—Émilienne d'Alençon. © Roger-Viollet

p. 43—Marthe Davelli, Opéra-Comique singer. © Albert Harlingue / Roger-Viollet

p. 44—Jeanne Dirys wearing a hat designed by Gabrielle Chanel, *Comœdia illustré*, March 1, 1911. Cover by Paul Iribe. Document of the Historical Library of the City of Paris. © Roger-Viollet. © ADAGP, Paris 2010

p. 47—Edgar Degas (1834–1917), *At the Milliner's*, 1883, pastel, 31.4 × 33.3 in. (79.9 × 84.8 cm). Madrid, Thyssen-Bornemisza Museum. © Museo Thyssen-Bornemisza, Madrid

p. 48—Henri Matisse (1869–1954), *Portrait of Madame Matisse*, 1912, oil on canvas, 57 × 38 in. (145 × 97 cm). Saint Petersburg, Hermitage Museum. © Estate of H. Matisse, Paris. © akg-images / Erich Lessing

p. 49—Henri Matisse (1869–1954), *Woman with a Hat*, 1905, oil on canvas, 31 × 25 in. (81 × 65 cm). San Francisco, San Francisco Museum of Modern Art. © Estate of H. Matisse, Paris / Artists Rights Society (ARS), New York. © SFMOMA

p. 50—Gabrielle Chanel wearing her own designs: a hat decorated with a black plume and a hat decorated with a white plume, *Comœdia illustré*, October 1, 1910. Document of the Historical Library of the City of Paris. © Roger-Viollet

p. 51—Hat designed by Gabrielle Chanel, *Comœdia illustré*, first Chanel cover, September 15th, 1910. Document of the Historical Library of the City of Paris. © Roger-Viollet

p. 52—Gabrielle Chanel in front of her first shop in Deauville, with her aunt Adrienne. Private collection. © Rights reserved

p. 54—Chanel in Biarritz, 1920. © Bernstein-Grüber collection

p. 55—Gabrielle Chanel in front of her first shop in Deauville, with a friend (on her left) wearing one of her designs, 1913. Private collection. © Rights reserved

p. 56—Pablo Picasso (1881–1973), *The Bathers*, Biarritz, summer 1918, oil on canvas, 10.3 × 8.5 in. (26.3 × 21.7 cm). Paris, Musée Picasso. © RMN. © The Estate of Pablo Picasso , 2010. © RMN / Béatrice Hatala

p. 58—Three jersey designs by Gabrielle Chanel, *Les Élégances parisiennes*, May 1916. Document of the Library of Decorative Arts, Paris. © Bridgeman Giraudon

p. 61—Georges Braque (1882–1963), *Le Petit Éclaireur*, 1913, charcoal and collage, 36 × 25 in. (92 × 65 cm). Villeneuve-d'Ascq, Museum of Modern Art. © Aisa / Roger-Viollet

p. 62 left—"Teheran" coat by Chanel in beige jersey, American *Vogue*, February 1, 1917. © The Condé Nast Publications Ltd., New York

p. 62, center—Chanel shirtdress in beige jersey, American *Vogue*, November 1, 1919. Document of the Library of Decorative Arts, Paris. © The Condé Nast Publications Ltd., New York. © Suzanne Nagy

p. 62 right—Cécile Sorel in a Chanel outfit in Ludovic Halévy's play *L'Abbé Constantin*, American *Vogue*, May 1, 1918. Document of the Library of Decorative Arts, Paris. © The Condé Nast Publications Ltd., New York. © Suzanne Nagy

p. 64—Pierre Bonnard (1867–1947), *Portrait of Misia,* 1908, oil on canvas, Madrid, Thyssen-Bornemisza Museum. © Museo Thyssen-Bornemisza, Madrid. © ADAGP, Paris 2010

p. 66—Gabrielle Chanel, photograph, 1909. © Rights reserved

p. 67 left—The actress Cécile Sorel, photography by Reutling. © Roger-Viollet

p. 67 right—Pierre Bonnard (1867–1947), *Misia Godebska in Profile,* c. 1900, drawing, 15.5 × 10.8 in. (39.5 × 27.5 cm). Paris, Musée du Louvre, DAG (Orsay collection). © RMN (Musée d'Orsay) / Jean-Gilles Berizzi. © ADAGP, Paris 2010

p. 68—Portrait of Misia Sert with balloons. Photographer unknown. Private collection. © Rights reserved

p. 71 top—Pablo Picasso (1881–1973), *Self-portrait,* 1917, pencil, 25 × 19.4 in. (64 × 49.5 cm). Paris, Musée Picasso. ©RMN / Thierry Le Mage. © The Estate of Pablo Picasso, 2010

p. 71 bottom—Pablo Picasso (1881–1973), *Portrait of Olga Picasso,* 1921, red chalk, 39 × 35 in. (100 × 90 cm). Inscribed to his son Paul on December 1, 1963. © DACS / Bridgeman Giraudon. © The Estate of Pablo Picasso, 2010

pp. 72–73—Pablo Picasso (1881–1973), drop curtain for *Parade,* 1917, distemper, 34.77 × 56.59 ft. (10.60 × 17.25 m). Paris, National Museum of Modern Art, Centre Georges-Pompidou. © CNAC/MNAM, dist. RMN/ Christian Bahier/Philippe Migeat. © The Estate of Pablo Picasso, 2010

p. 74 top—Igor Stravinsky, José Maria Sert, Misia Sert, and Gabrielle Chanel at the Paris Fair, 1920. Basel, Paul Sacher Foundation, Igor Stravinsky Collection. © Paul Sacher Foundation, Basel

p. 74 bottom—Pablo Picasso (1881–1973), *Portrait of Igor Stravinsky,* May 24, 1920, graphite, 24.5 × 19 in. (62.4 × 48.5 cm). Paris, Musée Picasso. © RMN / Béatrice Hatala. © The Estate of Pablo Picasso, 2010

p. 75—Serge de Diaghilev, photograph. © Roger-Viollet

p. 77—Gabrielle Chanel with Henry Bernstein and his daughter in Uriage, 1918. © Collection Bernstein-Grüber

p. 78—Juan Gris (1887–1927), *Portrait of Josette Gris,* 1916, oil on panel, 46 × 29 in. (116 × 73 cm). Madrid, Museo Nacional Centro de Arte Reina Sofía. © Museo Nacional Centro de Arte Reina Sofía, Madrid.

p. 79—Juan Gris (1887–1927), *Self-portrait,* 1920–1921, pencil, 13 × 10 in. (33 × 25 cm). Paris, National Museum of Modern Art, Centre Georges-Pompidou. © Centre Pompidou collection, dist. RMN / Philippe Migeat

p. 80 left—Valentine Hugo (1887–1968), *Portrait of Raymond Radiguet,* 1921, lithograph, 19.8 × 15 in. (50.3 × 38.3 cm). Paris, National Museum of Modern Art, Centre Georges-Pompidou. © Centre Pompidou collection, dist. RMN / Philippe Migeat. © ADAGP, Paris 2010

p. 80 right—Pablo Picasso (1881–1973), *Portrait of Max Jacob,* 1943, graphite, 14.3 × 10.4 in. (36.5 × 26.6 cm). Paris, Musée Picasso. © RMN / Michèle Bellot. © The Estate of Pablo Picasso, 2010

p. 81—The "Group des Six" (Georges Auric in the drawing) and Jean Cocteau, 1931. © Studio Lipnitzki / Roger-Viollet

p. 82—Lucas Cranach the Elder (1472–1553), *Mary Magdalene,* 1525, oil on panel, 18 × 11 in. (48 × 31 cm). Cologne, Stadt Köln / Rheinisches Bildarchiv. © Stadt Köln / Rheinisches Bildarchiv

p. 84—Bottle of Chanel No. 5 perfume. © Daniel Jouanneau

p. 85—Pablo Picasso (1881–1973), *Bottle and Wine Glass on Table,* 1912, charcoal, ink, cut and pasted newspaper and graphite on paper, 24.5 × 18.7 in. (62.5 × 47.3 cm). New York, The Metropolitan Museum of Art. © The Metropolitan Museum of Art, dist. RMN / Image of the MMA. © The Estate of Pablo Picasso, 2010

p. 86—Sem (1863–1934), poster design for Chanel No. 5, drawing for *Élégance et création.* © Rights reserved

p. 88—Henri Laurens (1885–1954), *Bottle and Glass*, 1919, painted stone, 13 × 4 × 4.5 in. (34 × 11 × 11.5 cm). Acquired from Galerie Louise Leiris (Paris) in 1994. LaM, Lille Métropole Museum of modern art, contemporary art and art brut. Photo by Jacques Hoepffner

p. 89—Chanel perfumes: Gardénia (1925), Bois des îles (1926), Cuir de Russie (1927). © Didier Roy

pp. 90, 93—Haute couture collection, Fall–Winter 1922, Chanel coat in black crepe embroidered in point de Beauvais with colorful Russian friezes by Kitmir. Photos © Didier Roy

p. 94—Véra Sergine in Henry Bernstein's *Secret*, wearing a Chanel dress, *Femina*, April 1, 1919. © Wyndham / Rights reserved

p. 95—Madame Jacques Porel wearing a Chanel dress, French *Vogue*, September 1, 1922. Document of the Library of Decorative Arts, Paris. © *Vogue* Paris

p. 96—Antigone brought by two guards before Creon, Greek vase from Lucania, c. 380–370 BCE. London, British Museum. © The Trustees of the British Museum

p. 98—Charles Dullin in the role of Creon, in Jean Cocteau's *Antigone*, 1922. Private collection. © Rights reserved

p. 101—Chanel costumes for Jean Cocteau's *Antigone*: Antigone and Ismene. French *Vogue*, February 1, 1923. © *Vogue* France

p. 102—Marie Laurencin (1885–1956), *Portrait of Gabrielle Chanel*, 1923, oil on canvas, 36 × 29 in. (92 × 73 cm). Paris, Musée de l'Orangerie. © RMN / Hervé Lewandowski. © ADAGP, Paris 2010

p. 104—Program for the ballet *Le Train Bleu*, Théâtre des Champs-Élysées, 1924. Document of the library and museum of the Opéra, Paris. © BnF, Paris

p. 105—Pablo Picasso (1881–1973), *Two Women Running on the Beach (The Race)*, summer 1922, gouache on wood, 13 × 17 in. (34 × 42.5 cm). Paris, Musée Picasso. © RMN / Jean-Gilles Berizzi. © The Estate of Pablo Picasso, 2010

pp. 106, 107—Jean Cocteau with Lydia Sokolova, Anton Dolin, Léon Woïzikovsky and Bronislava Nijinska. Lydia Sokolova playing Perlouse and Anton Dolin in the role of Beau Gosse. Photographs of the ballet *Le Train Bleu*, 1924. © Getty Images

p. 108—Amedeo Modigliani (1884–1920), *Portrait of Henri Laurens*, 1915, oil on canvas, 34.7 × 45.5 in. (88.3 × 115.8 cm). Lucerne, Museum Collection Rosengart. © Museum Collection Rosengart

p. 109—Serge Lifar, 1925. © Archives of the City of Lausanne, Serge Lifar collection

p. 110—Madame Varda in a Chanel evening gown of white georgette crepe. Photograph by Edward Steichen, American *Vogue*, October 1, 1924. © The Condé Nast Publications Ltd. Permission of Johanna Steichen

p. 113—Marion Morehouse in a blue crepe Chanel evening dress with silk fringes. Photograph by Edward Steichen, American *Vogue*, October 1, 1924. © The Condé Nast Publications Ltd. Permission of Johanna Steichen

p. 114 left—Chanel suit of plain and printed crepella, French *Vogue*, April 1, 1925. © *Vogue* France

p. 114 right—Chanel evening gown in white georgette crepe, French *Vogue*, April 1, 1925. © *Vogue* France

p. 116—"Primavera," wall painting from Stabiae, first century BCE. Naples, National Museum. © Scala, Florence

p. 117—Chanel black sequined suit, 1926. Photograph by Irving Penn. © The Estate of Irving Penn

p. 118—Fernand Léger (1881–1955), *Composition*, 1920, pencil and gouache, 13 × 9.6 in. (34 × 24.5 cm). Frankfurt am Main, Graphische Sammlung, Städel Museum. © U. Edelmann-Städel Museum / Artothek. © ADAGP, Paris 2010

p. 119 top—1925 Ford model. © Roger-Viollet

p. 119 bottom—Black Chanel dress, French *Vogue*, November 1926. © *Vogue* France. © Corbis

p. 120—Ina Claire in a Chanel gown in embroidered tulle with beads and sequins. Photograph by Edward Steichen, American *Vogue*, May 1, 1926. © Corbis / The Condé Nast Publications Ltd. Permission of Johanna Steichen

p. 121—Marion Morehouse in a black crepe Chanel gown with an overskirt of fringe embroidered with sequins. Photograph by Edward Steichen, American *Vogue*, May 1, 1926. © Corbis / The Condé Nast Publications Ltd. Permission of Johanna Steichen

p. 122—Jean Cocteau, 1926. © Henri Martinie / Roger-Viollet

p. 125—Pablo Picasso (1881–1973), *Portrait of Jean Cocteau*, 1917, graphite, 10.3 x 7.6 in. (26.3 x 19.4 cm). Stéphane Dermit collection, on loan to the Maison Jean-Cocteau, Milly-la-Forêt. © The Estate of Pablo Picasso, 2010

p. 126—Jean Hugo, sets for Jean Cocteau's *Orphée*, *L'Art vivant*, August 1, 1926. Paris, Historical Library of the City of Paris. © Roger-Viollet. © ADAGP, Paris 2010

p. 128—Interior of the Chanel shop at 31 Rue Cambon, Paris. Model wearing a gown from the 1927 collection. Photograph by Adolphe de Meyer, *Harper's Bazaar*, April 1927. © *Harper's Bazaar*

p. 131 left—Chanel gown in black taffeta, French *Vogue*, May 1928. Paris, Library of Decorative Arts. © *Vogue* France. © Suzanne Nagy

p. 131 right—Chanel gown in rose georgette crepe. French *Vogue*, September 1929. Paris, Library of Decorative Arts. © *Vogue* France. © Suzanne Nagy

p. 132—Chanel gown in apricot organdy with beadwork, American *Vogue*, April 12th, 1930. © Corbis / The Condé Nast Publications Ltd.

p. 133—Chanel gown in blue silk tulle with sequins, 1927–1928. Photograph by Irving Penn. © The Estate of Irving Penn

p. 134—Ina Claire in a black Chanel suit trimmed with red fox. Photograph by Von Horn, French *Vogue*, January 1931. Document of UFAC, Paris. © *Vogue* Paris / Von Horn

p. 135—Attributed to El Greco (1541–1614), *Woman with Ermine*, 1577–1578, oil on canvas, 24 x 20 in. (62 x 50 cm). Glasgow, Pollok House, Glasgow Museums and Art Galleries. © Culture and Sport Glasgow (Museums) / The Bridgeman Art Library

p. 136—Saint Modeste, north portal of Chartres Cathedral, thirteenth century. © Roger-Viollet

p. 137—Chanel evening gown in spring green chiffon. Photograph by Hoyningen-Huene, American *Vogue*, February 15th, 1931. © The Condé Nast Publications Ltd

p. 138—Lady Abdy in a white silk chiffon evening gown by Chanel, American *Vogue*, April 1931. © Corbis / The Condé Nast Publications Ltd.

p. 139—Henri Matisse (1869–1954), *Woman with a Madras Hat*, 1929, oil on canvas, 71 x 60 in. (180 x 152 cm). Private collection. © Matisse archives, collection of Claude Duthuit. © The Estate of Henri Matisse

p. 140—Chanel in London, 1931. Photograph published in *The Smithsonian*, May 1971. Paris, American Library. © Suzanne Nagy

p. 143—Eaton Hall, east facade. © *Country Life*

p. 144—Lady Pamela Smith in a Chanel evening gown of pale pink lace with an ostrich boa. Photograph by Adolphe de Meyer, *Harper's Bazaar*, June 1932. © *Harper's Bazaar*

p. 146—Gloria Swanson dressed by Chanel in the film *Tonight or Never*, 1931. New York, The Museum of Modern Art / Stills Archive. © Academy Foundation

p. 149—Édouard Vuillard (1868–1940), *Portrait of Countess Anna de Noailles*, c. 1932, charcoal on canvas, 43 x 50 in. (110 x 128 cm). Paris, Musée du Louvre, DAG (Orsay collection). © RMN (Musée d'Orsay) / Jean-Gilles Berizzi

p. 150—Colette in her beauty shop on Rue de Miromesnil, 1932. © Studio Lipnitzki / Roger-Viollet

p. 152—Robert Delaunay (1885–1941), *Portrait of Iliazd*, 1922, pencil. New York, The Museum of Modern Art. © 2010. Digital Image, The Museum of Modern Art, New York / Scala, Florence. © L&M Services

p. 153—Pablo Picasso (1881–1973), engraving for *Afat*, 1938. Chanel collection. © The Estate of Pablo Picasso, 2010

p. 154 top—Knitting loom designed by Iliazd for the House of Chanel. Private collection. © Iliazd collection.

p. 154 bottom—Two testimonials for Iliazd issued by the House of Chanel. Private collection. © Iliazd collection.

p. 155—Chanel fabric samples. Private collection. © Iliazd collection.

p. 156—Drawing room in Gabrielle Chanel's townhouse at 29, Faubourg Saint-Honoré, Paris, published in *Art et Industrie*, February 1931. © Revue *Art et Industrie* / Rights reserved

pp. 159, 160—Two views of Chanel's apartment at 31 Rue Cambon, Paris. Dining room and drawing room. Photographs by Robert Doisneau. © Atelier Robert Doisneau

p. 162—La Pausa, Chanel's villa in Roquebrune, 1938. Photograph by Roger Schall. © Roger Schall, Paris

p. 163—Gabrielle Chanel with François Hugo and Maria Hugo de Gramont and their son Georges in the old fig tree. Below: Pierre Colle and a lady friend, 1938. Photograph by Roger Schall. © Roger Schall, Paris

p. 164—Pierre Reverdy (1889–1960), poem taken from *Cravates de chanvre*, illustrated by Picasso, 1922. Unique copy decorated with watercolors. © The Estate of Pablo Picasso, 2010. © Rights reserved

p. 165—Juan Gris (1887–1927), *Portrait of Pierre Reverdy*, 1918, pencil on cardboard, 23 × 16 in. (60 × 40.5 cm). Gift. of Mrs. Pierre Reverdy, 1975. © Rights reserved

p. 166—Pierre Reverdy, 1928. Photograph by Thomas Bouchard. Private collection. © Thomas Bouchard

p. 167—Jacques Lipchitz (1891–1973), *Portrait of Gabrielle Chanel*, 1922, bronze. Photograph by Ali Elai. Private collection. © Ali Elai, New York. © The Estate of Jacques Lipchitz

p. 168—Cassandre (1901–1968), *Portrait of Gabrielle Chanel*, 1942, oil on canvas. BALENCIAGA company archives. © Olivier Saillant. © Mouron. Cassandre. License number 2010-28-06-04

p. 169—Cassandre (1901–1968), *Portrait of Pierre Reverdy*, 1943, oil on canvas. © Mouron. Cassandre. License number 2010-28-06-04

pp. 170–171—*Maxims and Aphorisms of Gabrielle Chanel*, graphic design by Jean Picart Le Doux, French *Vogue*, September 1938. © *Vogue* France

p. 172—Gentile Bellini (c. 1429–1507), *Procession of the True Cross in Saint Mark's Square*, 1496, oil on canvas. Venice, Gallerie dell'Accademia. © Scala Archives, Florence

p. 174—Gabrielle Chanel in Venice, French *Vogue*, October 1936. Document of the Library of Decorative Arts, Paris. © Suzanne Nagy

p. 176—Misia Sert in Venice wearing a Chanel suit, summer 1947. Photograph by Horst. © The Estate of Horst P. Horst, New York

p. 177—Misia Sert in Venice, 1947. Photograph by Horst. © The Estate of Horst P. Horst, New York

p. 178—The Empress Theodora, detail of the mosaic in the choir of Saint Vitale, Ravenna, before 547. © Skira archives

pp. 180, 181—Necklace in patinated vermeil composed of one hundred and twenty-one lion's heads, 1960s. Chanel jewelry executed by Robert Goossens. Chanel collection. © Didier Roy

p. 182—Gabrielle Chanel and Fulco di Verdura, 1937. Photograph by Lipnitzki. © Lipnitzki / Roger-Viollet

p. 183 top—Pablo Picasso (1881–1973), *Portrait of Count Étienne de Beaumont*, 1925, pencil on paper and eraser marks, 24 × 19 in. (60 × 48 cm). Private collection (archival photos). © The Estate of Pablo Picasso, 2010

p. 183 bottom—Cuff bracelets in black and white Bakelite decorated with a cruciform motif in glass and paste gemstones, 1960s. Chanel jewelry executed by Robert Goossens. Chanel collection. © Didier Roy

p. 184—Gabrielle Chanel preparing her Fine Jewelry exhibition, 1932, pen and ink drawing by Christian Bérard. Private collection. Photo Jacqueline Hyde, Paris

p. 185—Princess J.-L. de Faucigny-Lucinge, Madame Ralli, and Baron de Gunzburg visiting Chanel's Fine Jewelry exhibition, 1932. Photograph by Kertész, French *Vogue*, January 1933. Document of UFAC, Paris. © Jacqueline Hyde, Paris

pp. 186, 187 bottom—"Noeud" necklace and "Franges" bracelet from the Bijoux de Diamants collection designed by Gabrielle Chanel in 1932. © Robert Bresson, "Bijoux de Diamants," *Mademoiselle Chanel*, 1932

p. 187 top—Cover of the Bijoux de Diamants press release. Chanel collection. © Chanel

p. 188—Chanel's jewelry showcase, 31 Rue Cambon, Paris, 1938. Photograph by Roger Schall. © Roger Schall, Paris

p. 189—Peter Paul Rubens (1577–1640), *Portrait of Helena Fourment*, c. 1630, oil on panel, 29 x 22 in. (75 x 56 cm). Amsterdam, Rijksmuseum. © Rijksmuseum collection, Amsterdam

p. 190—Chanel's jewelry showcase, 31 Rue Cambon, Paris, 1938. Photograph by Roger Schall. © Roger Schall, Paris

p. 191—Necklaces in gilded metal with camellia motifs in red, blue, and green glass. 1938. Chanel jewelry executed by Gripoix. Chanel collection. © Didier Roy

p. 192—Necklace in gilded metal and red and green glass and white pearls, early 1970s; reliquary cross in gilt bronze with engraved setting of a religious figure on both sides, 1960s; cross in gilt brass decorated with seven tiles in red and green glass, 1965. Chanel jewelry executed by Robert Goossens. Chanel collection. Photos © Didier Roy

p. 193—Chanel playing the accordion. Photograph by François Kollar, *Harper's Bazaar*, September 15, 1937. Private collection (photo print 1987, copyright © Jean-Michel Kollar)

p. 194—Gabrielle Chanel, 1937. Photograph by Lipnitzki. © Lipnitzki-Roger-Viollet

p. 196—Chanel tailored suit in black ciré satin. Photograph by Hoyningen-Huene, French *Vogue*, May 1933. © George Hoyningen-Huene © *Vogue* Paris, May 1933

p. 197—Chanel black satin dress with white satin bib collar. Photograph by Hoyningen-Huene, American *Vogue*, September 1, 1934. © The Condé Nast Publications Ltd.

p. 198—François Clouet (c. 1510–1572), *Elisabeth of Austria*, 1571, three pencils. Paris, Bibliothèque nationale de France, print and photography department. © BnF, Paris

p. 199—Gabrielle Chanel, 1939. Photograph by Hoyningen-Huene. © Getty Images

p. 201—Paul Iribe (1883–1935), Gabrielle Chanel as Marianne. Cover of *Le Témoin*, October 14, 1934. © ADAGP, Paris 2010. © Kharbine-Tapabor collection

p. 202—Lucas Cranach the Younger (1515–1586), *Portrait of a Lady*, 1564, oil on panel, 33 x 25 in. (83 x 64 cm). Vienna, Kunsthistorisches Museum. © Kunsthistorisches Museum, Vienna

p. 204 left—Drawing of two Chanel designs by Christian Bérard, French *Vogue*, October 1, 1937. Document of UFAC, Paris. © *Vogue* France. © ADAGP, Paris 2010

p. 204 right—Christian Bérard and Gabrielle Chanel in Monte-Carlo, 1938. Photograph by Roger Schall. © Roger Schall, Paris

p. 205—Chanel dresses in navy blue tulle and white-embroidered black lace. Photograph by André Durst, American *Vogue*, April 1, 1936. © The Condé Nast Publications Ltd.

p. 206—Chanel dress in white tulle. Photograph by André Durst, American *Vogue*, June 15, 1938. © The Condé Nast Publications Ltd.

p. 207—A Chanel dress of white sequin-embroidered lace and net, another of black and white lace. Photograph by André Durst, American *Vogue*, October 15, 1936. © The Condé Nast Publications Ltd.

p. 208—Chanel dress in pink tulle with black and gold lamé. Photograph by Hoyningen-Huene, *Harper's Bazaar*, November 1937. © *Harper's Bazaar*

p. 209—Chanel dress in white crepe and silver brocade bodice. Photograph by Horst, French *Vogue*, September 1937. Document of UFAC, Paris. © Horst P. Horst. © *Vogue* Paris, August 1937

p. 210—Christian Bérard (1902–1949), Gabrielle Chanel in black tulle dresses with ostrich plumes and sequined bows, French *Vogue*, July 1937. Document of UFAC, Paris. © ADAGP, Paris 2010

p. 211—Two models in Chanel tulle gowns. Bas-relief by Alberto Giacometti. Setting by Jean-Michel Frank. Photograph by Man Ray, *Harper's Bazaar*, September 1, 1937. © *Harper's Bazaar*. © ADAGP, Paris 2010

p. 212—Jean Cocteau's *Knights of the Round Table*, Théâtre de l'Œuvre, October 1937. Costumes by Chanel. Lucien Pascal, Any Marène, and Samson Fainsilber. Photograph by Lipnitzki. Photos © Lipnitzki / Roger-Viollet

p. 213—Jean Cocteau's *Oedipus Rex*, after Sophocles, Théâtre-Antoine, July 1937, with Michel Saïanov and Lady Abdy in Chanel costumes. Photograph by Lipnitzki. © Lipnitzki / Roger-Viollet

p. 214—Gabrielle Chanel and Salvador Dalí at 31 Rue Cambon, Paris, 1938. Photograph by Roger Schall. © Roger Schall, Paris

p. 215—The ballet *Bacchanale*, costumes designed by Dalí and executed by Chanel, 1939. Photograph by Horst. © The Estate of Horst P. Horst, New York

p. 216—Luchino Visconti and Gabrielle Chanel, 1938. Private collection (archival photos)

p. 217—Jean Renoir and Nora Grégor in a Chanel dress in Renoir's film *The Rules of the Game*, 1939. © Roger-Viollet

p. 218—Gabrielle Chanel standing between coromandel screens in her apartment at 31 Rue Cambon. Photograph by Lipnitzki. © Lipnitzki / Roger-Viollet

p. 221—Chanel with Valentine Lawford in her 1948 MG; in the background, Baroness Maggie Van Zuylen. Oyster Bay (New York), 1951. Photograph by Horst. © The Horst P. Horst Estate, New York)

p. 222—Marie-Hélène Arnaud in a navy blue tailored Chanel jersey. Photograph by Henry Clarke, French *Vogue*, March 1954. © ADAGP, Paris 2010

p. 225—Gabrielle Chanel on the staircase at 31 Rue Cambon, Paris. Photograph by Suzy Parker, French *Vogue*, March 1954. © ADAGP, Paris 2010

p. 226—Gabrielle Chanel in her apartment at 31 Rue Cambon, Paris, 1954. Photograph by Alexander Liberman. Private collection. © Alexander Liberman

p. 227—Gabrielle Chanel. Photograph by Cecil Beaton, April 1965. © Condé Nast Archive / Corbis

p. 228—Chanel shirtdress in red jersey, American *Vogue*, January 1955. Document of American *Vogue*, Paris. © The Condé Nast Publications Ltd.

p. 229—Model Joanna McCormick in a Chanel tailored suit in white silk and gold brocade with navy blue and gold velvet trimmings. Photograph by Henry Clarke, French Vogue, April 1957. *Vogue* Paris collection. © ADAGP, Paris 2010. © 2008 Getty Images

p. 230—Model Marie-Hélène Arnaud in a Chanel print dress in silk muslin from the Spring to Summer 1957 Haute Couture collection. Photograph by Henry Clarke, French *Vogue*, May 1957. © ADAGP, Paris 2010. © *Vogue* France

p. 231—Sandro Botticelli (1445–1510), *The Birth of Venus*, c. 1482, oil on canvas (detail). Florence, Uffizi Gallery. © Dagli-Orti

p. 232—Chanel dress in silk organdy. Photograph by Guy Bourdin, French *Vogue*, May 1960. © The Estate of Guy Bourdin / Art + Commerce

p. 233—Chanel dress in black muslin and sequins. Photograph by Henry Clarke, French *Vogue*, March 1961. © ADAGP, Paris 2010. © *Vogue* France

p. 234—Model Marie-Hélène Arnaud in a tailored suit from the Spring–Summer 1959 Haute Couture collection in black tweed braided with black silk, blouse in white surah. Photograph by Henry Clarke, French *Vogue*, April 1959. © Henry Clarke, Musée Galliera-ADAGP, Paris 2010

p. 235—Model Paule de Mérindol in a tailored suit from the Spring–Summer 1959 Haute Couture collection in beige tweed trimmed with navy grosgrain, standing in front of the shop at 31 Rue Cambon. © Roger-Viollet

p. 236—Romy Schneider in a gold lamé tunic dress by Chanel in the Visconti film *Boccaccio '70*, 1962. © Éditions de l'Étoile, Cahiers du cinéma / Paul Ronald

p. 237—Romy Schneider at a fitting with Gabrielle Chanel in the studio at 31 Rue Cambon. Photograph by Giancarlo Botti, 1960. © Giancarlo Botti

p. 238—Chanel suit, jacket and pants in gold and chartreuse lamé brocade. Photograph by Henry Clarke, French *Vogue*, April 1969. © ADAGP, Paris 2010. © *Vogue* France

p. 239—Dragon robe, embroidery on satin weave silk, late-eighteenth to mid-nineteenth century. London, Victoria and Albert Museum. © Scala archives

p. 240—Model Dorothy McGowan in a Chanel tailored suit from the Fall–Winter 1960 Haute Couture collection in white tweed with navy wool braided trim. Photograph by William Klein, French *Vogue*, October 1960. © William Klein, 1960

p. 242—Gabrielle Chanel and model Muriel Maxwell, wearing an outfit inspired by Watteau. Photograph by Horst, American *Vogue*, September 15, 1939. © The Estate of Horst P. Horst, New York

p. 243—Bottle of Coco perfume. © Daniel Jouanneau

p. 244—Inès de la Fressange in a white silk Chanel ensemble from the 1985 Spring–Summer Haute Couture collection. Photograph by Horst, French *Vogue*, October 1985. © The Estate of Horst P. Horst

p. 245—Antoine Watteau (1684–1721), *Pierrot, Formerly Known as Gilles*, oil on canvas, 72 × 59 in. (184 × 149 cm). Paris, Musée du Louvre. © RMN / Jean-Gilles Berizzi

p. 246—Raincoat dating from the early eighteenth century, American *Vogue*, October 2007. © Rights reserved

p. 247—Raquel Zimmermann in a Chanel dress in light pink taffeta from the Fall–Winter 2007 haute couture collection. Photograph by David Sims, American *Vogue*, October 2007. © David Sims

Translated from the French by Antony Shugaar

Designer: Sylvie Legastelois, with Jennyfer Moulin
Editors: Brigitte Govignon and Isabelle Dartois
Photo research and permissions: Annabelle Biau, Carole Daprey, and Cécile Goddet-Dirles
Production managers: Cécile Vandenbroucque, Florent Roger, and Éric Peyronnet
Proofreading: Marion Lacroix

English-language edition:
Project Manager: Aiah Rachel Wieder
Designer: Shawn Dahl, dahlimama inc
Production Managers: Jacquie Poirier and Erin Vandeveer

Library of Congress Control Number: 2011281833
ISBN: 978-0-8109-9694-6

Printed and bound in China
10 9 8

Abrams books are available at special discounts when purchased in quantity for premiums and
promotions as well as fundraising or educational use. Special editions can also be created to
specification. For details, contact specialsales@abramsbooks.com or the address below.

ABRAMS The Art of Books
195 Broadway, New York, NY 10007
abramsbooks.com